D0756184

Molaise

Abbot of Leighlin and Hermit of Holy Island

The life and legacy of Saint Laisren in Ireland and Scotland

Colum Kenny

Morrigan

Morrigan
an imprint of
Morigna MediaCo Teo
Killala
County Mayo
Ireland

©1998 Colum Kenny

ISBN 0 907677 67 3

Design & Origination by Identikit
Printed in Ireland by Betaprint

Front cover: illustration (from a photo by John O'Neill)
is of a stained glass window (c.1933) by Catherine O'Brien in
Old Leighlin Cathedral, Co.Carlow.
Back cover: Holy Island from Dún Fionn, Arran
(photo courtesy Colin Cowley).

All rights reserved. No part of this publication may be copied,
reproduced or transmitted in any form or by any means,
without the permission of the copyright owner.

Contents

Acknowledgements

During the preparation of this book many people on the Isle of Arran and in Co. Carlow and elsewhere have extended kindnesses to the author.

The librarians, keepers and archivists who have been of assistance include those of the Argyll and Bute District Archives; Arran Banner; Arran Estate Office; Arran Library; Bray Public Library, Co. Wicklow; British Library, London; Bibliothèque Nationale, Paris; Bibliothèque Royale, Brussels; Carlow Chamber of Commerce; Department of Arts, Culture and the Gaeltacht, Ireland (Office of Public Works); Committee for Aerial Photography, University of Cambridge; Dublin City University; Gilbert Library, Dublin; Historic Monuments and Buildings, Belfast; Historic Scotland; Hunterian Museum, Glasgow; Hydrographic Office, Taunton; Irish Architectural Archive; Isle of Arran Museum; Isle of Arran Tourist Board; King's Inns; Leighlin Cathedral; Mitchell Library, Glasgow; National Archives, Dublin; National Gallery of Ireland; National Library of Ireland; National Library of Scotland; National Museum of Ireland; National Museums of Scotland; Naval History Museum, London; Prinknash Abbey, Gloucester; Registry of Deeds, Dublin; Representative Church Body Library, Dublin; Royal Irish Academy; Saint Patrick's College, Maynooth; Samye Ling Tibetan Centre, Eskdalemuir; Scotland's Lighthouse Museum, Fraserburgh; The John Rylands Research Institute, University of Manchester; Trinity College Dublin; Universities Federation for Animal Welfare; University College Dublin; University of Glasgow.

Thanks are due to Fr James Smyth S.J. for his translations. The Glasgow University Archaeological Research Division met me and allowed me to read and to cite an unpublished report by Ms Rachel Harry on GUARD's preliminary investigation of sites of historical interest on Holy Island. Extracts from a survey of Carlow folklore collected by schoolchildren in 1938 are published by permission of the head of the Department of Irish Folklore, University College Dublin.

Mr Colin Cowley, formerly of Lamlash and now of Liverpool, wrote to me a number of times following the publication in the *Arran Banner* of a letter from me about my research. His correspondence, as well as his *Arran Book File* and *Annals of Arran*, (works which have had too limited a circulation), were most useful. Many other individuals have also assisted me, including in Leighlinbridge Fr John Aughney, Dean Cecil Faull, Ms Mary MacDonald, Mr and Mrs Johnny Murphy, Mr Martin Nevin and others; on the Isle of Arran Rev. Andrew Barrie of St Molios, Mr Angus Adamson of Corriecravie, Mrs Sheena and Mr Jim Bannatyne of North Feorline, Mr Bill McLaughlin of Whiting Bay and others; Lama Yeshe, the director of the Holy Island Project, and the caretakers and community of Holy Island who facilitated my visits there; Mr Kenneth Barnes of Lincoln; Ms Kay Kirk, formerly Kay Morris, of Dumfriesshire; Mr Kenneth Hall of Ayr who provided old postcards of Arran, one of which is reproduced below; Ms Deirdre McCartin; Dr Bríona Nic Dhiarmada for a translation; Ani Rinchen Khandro and Mr Nick Jennings of Samye Ling; Mr John O'Neill of the Samye Trust, Dublin, for his generous advice and assistance.

Finally, may I express my gratitude to Catherine Curran and to our sons, Oisín, Conor and Samuel, who have supported my work and have borne with tolerance my preoccupations. I hope that I support them and bear theirs as willingly. To these and to all others who have helped me in any way I am grateful.

Matrix of the seal of the chapter of Leighlin, [c.1300AD].
National Museum, R.3057. Repr. from Dowling, Annals.

Introduction

ONE PERSON connects startling plans for a modern holistic retreat centre in the Firth of Clyde with an ancient cathedral and holy well in Co. Carlow; he also connects the forgotten Irish-Scots kingdom of Dál Riada with an order of Tibetan monks who have found refuge in Britain. He is Laisren.

Known today in Ireland as 'Laserian' and in Scotland as 'Molaise' and 'Molios', which are derivative forms of his original Celtic name, he is the saint of Holy Island, Arran, and of Leighlin in Leinster. Laisren passed away about 638 but is still being recalled at the end of the twentieth century.

In Ireland and Scotland during the middle ages Laisren was considered to have led a very distinguished life. His former Scottish hermitage was long visited by pilgrims who left their mark in the form of Christian crosses scratched on rocks. Holy Island has recently been acquired by Buddhists who intend to make it a location for inter-faith meetings and meditation. They have already established a small community in the former light-house station and farmhouse. Elsewhere on the island are the ruins of a medieval Christian foundation, which may have been home to that 'religious order of Molaise' ('órd ríaghalt mholaisi') which was founded by Ranald, king of the isles and Argyll (rí Insi Gall agus oirire Gaoidheal), but about which little is now known.[1]

The Buddhists who own Holy Island have received much international attention in the media and their plans are being supported by many people, including Christians of various churches. Questions are being asked about Laisren not only in Scotland but also in Ireland, where there is a growing interest in the saints of the Celtic church and where Laisren has recently inspired the writing of a new sung-Mass in the Irish language.

In Co. Carlow the cathedral of St 'Laserian' at Leighlin (pronounced 'Locklin') is an intriguing building which stands at the heart of the old Gaelic kingdom of Leinster. One of the legendary great trees of Ireland is reputed to have grown nearby. Here, in the valley of the stately River Barrow, Laisren founded a community of 1,500 people which was later remembered principally for its healing abilities. Today both the Church of Ireland and Roman Catholic authorities cooperate locally in the celebration of his annual feast-day. Cooperation was unthinkable in the bitter climate of former years.

It was in 1974 that this author became aware that there were Tibetan Buddhists in Scotland and that they had created near Lockerbie a community called Samye Ling. They came to my attention through a footnote in the remarkable writings of Thomas Merton, an American Cistercian who had reached out to Asian religious practitioners before his untimely death. The Buddhists' centre of activity in Scotland has expanded steadily and when I learnt that they had acquired Holy Island in 1992 I was intrigued. My curiosity eventually led me to investigate why their island has come to be regarded as sacred and the result of that search is this book.

Who was the abbot of Leighlin and hermit of Holy Island who has allowed Christians and Buddhists to find common ground? Laisren himself was born in the second half of the sixth century. The name which he was given at birth was once quite common in Ireland. Its root, 'las', means 'flame'. Those who bore it were sometimes affectionately known as 'Molaise' (traditionally pronounced 'moh-lash-eh'), the Gaelic 'mo' meaning 'my'. Early scribes referred to Laisren as 'a victorious flame', as well as 'gentle abbot of Leighlin'.[2]

Laisren's ancestors belonged to the Ulaid septs of north-eastern Ireland, some of whom embarked on the creation of permanent settlements among the islands and highlands across the sea. His father is said to have been a local king in Ulster and his mother was the daughter of Aedán mac Gabráin, the most powerful leader of his day in what is now western Scotland and the isles. St Colum Cille, one of the great figures of the Celtic church, became an ally of Laisren's maternal grandfather. In the first recorded Christian ordination of any Gaelic king, Colum Cille gave Aedán his special blessing. Laisren himself avoided high worldly office. He decided to become a monk instead of succeeding his father as one of the kings of Ulster.

As a young man Laisren made his way to Holy Island, where he is thought to have lived for some years as a hermit in a cave. Rearing up out of the sea lanes at the mouth of the Clyde estuary, and visible from both Scotland and Ireland, is the massive cone of Ailsa Craig (popularly known as 'Paddy's Milestone'). Not far north in that same estuary is Holy Island, which from the Scottish mainland looks like it is physically attached to the much larger island of Arran but which actually sits in the mouth of Lamlash Bay, its rocky peak of Mullach Mór rising to over 1,000 feet. The great natural harbour of Lamlash, sheltered as it is by Holy Island, takes its name from the saint, 'Molaise'.

Laisren eventually gave up his island home and went to Rome to study. Later he journeyed to Leighlin, where he was to serve as both abbot and bishop. He is reputed to have played a significant role in the adoption within Ireland of the controversial Roman method of dating Easter. The stories about his life which came to be handed down in writing and in folklore are examined below and they shed light on many aspects of Gaelic society, including its attitude towards religion, death and even sex. There are also shadowy intimations of the stresses which existed between the druidic order and Christians, as well as clues to the elusive locations of the great annual Fair of Carman and the famous plain of Mag n-Ailbe.

From a study of the surviving medieval account of Laisren's life, and from other ancient sources, it is clear that Laisren was a remarkable man who was believed to have miraculous powers. He long remained a figure of popular devotion. However, he had a darker side which was reflected in his extreme penitential practices and in his attitude towards his sister, whom he is said to have cursed for becoming pregnant by a monk. When he himself died, perhaps in a dispute over druidic practices, he was honoured by what was reputed to be the third of the three most exalted burials that had taken place in Ireland in the Christian period. The others were those of St Patrick and of St Mochuda.

For their part the people of Arran long believed that he was buried on that island and the location of his reputed grave was for centuries marked by a unique carved slab which is now built into the wall of the modern Presbyterian church of 'Saint Molios'. From Molaise's 'grave' on the western side of Arran to the eastern shore opposite Holy Island there once ran a well-trodden 'Pilgrims' Way', which has been neglected in recent times.

After his death Laisren soon came to be regarded as a saint. From an early date, in both Ireland and Scotland, his feast-day has been celebrated on 18 April each year. In this way, amongst others, Laisren of Leighlin and Arran is distinguished from other Irish saints of the same name, including Laisren of Devenish and Laisren of Inishmurray.

The fullest account of Laisren's life dates in its present form from the twelfth or thirteenth century. Known as 'the Salamanca manuscript', having been discovered in that city, it is today kept in Brussels and is referred to below as 'S'. Two similar but later versions of his 'Life' are those passed on by Thomas Arthur ('A') and Henry Fitzsimon ('F'). I am grateful to Fr James Smyth S.J. of Belvedere College, Dublin, for having completed at my request the first English translation of the complete Salamanca manuscript and of sections of the Fitzsimon version and other documents.[3]

It is usual for such manuscript 'lives' to have been derived from earlier versions or exemplars, either oral or written, but a later scribe may have omitted or changed details as thought fit. These three similar accounts of Laisren do not include certain interesting stories concerning his life and death, which are related elsewhere and which include tales emphasising the strict or penitential side of his nature. Nor do they mention what is said to have been his leading role in the controversy over Easter. For such information I have looked to some other and older sources.

As is common in the case of medieval 'lives', those of Laisren include certain miraculous incidents, as well as anachronistic details which indicate that they were not written down in their present form until centuries after the saint's death. While such medieval chronicles or 'lives' of the saints may be hagiographical, fantastic and otherwise unsatisfactory, they do allow us to catch a glimpse of how certain saints were regarded subsequently. Stories attached themselves to particular holy persons and continued to be associated with them, rather than with anyone else, no matter how much each 'life' adopted certain formulas or conventions.[4]

Moreover, it is not only by texts that the dearly departed are commemorated. Folklore too preserves stories about them and folk practices honour their names. There are today holy wells both at Leighlin and on Holy Island which are associated with 'Molaise' and which have long been visited by those who respect the saint's memory. The cave where the saint is believed to have dwelt in Scotland is also a sacred place and is treated with respect by its new Buddhist owners. A steady stream of visitors travels to Arran to make their way by small boat across Lamlash Bay to Holy Island. Among them recently was a reporter for one leading British Sunday newspaper. Reflecting on the current plan to build a retreat centre there, he wrote in a prominent article that, 'it may not be so far removed from what St Molaise had in mind when he arrived on Holy Island in the sixth century'.[5]

What exactly 'St Molaise had in mind', or actually did, we shall never know for certain. The writing of history depends on surviving records and accounts which are imperfect and may be false. Historians must be circumspect and be conscious of the fact that each generation creates its own social and cultural 'imaginary' out of those fragments of the past and interpretations of the past which it inherits or recalls. The final chapter below examines how Laisren has been remembered over the centuries and the author explains why he believes that his subject is still relevant today.

Each year on 18 April hundreds of people gather in Carlow to celebrate Laisren at their holy well and locals still drink its waters, which are thought to have curative properties. On Arran too he is remembered. There is cause to wonder who was this saint whose influence abides and whose role in the Celtic church was an important one. I attempt to answer that question in the following pages and in doing so reveal a figure whose life appears to have been both complex and inspiring and whose legacy for the present age is a vibrant one.

Folio from manuscript, 'Vita S. Lasriani'.
Courtesy Bibliothèque Royale, Brussels.

CHAPTER 1

Royal blood

L AISREN WAS born among people whose shifting loyalties straddled the present boundaries of Ireland and Scotland. He lived at a time when a gradual migration was taking place from the north of Ireland, a migration which was to give to Scotland its name, its Christian faith and its Gaelic tongue. Laisren inhabited a world of fluid borders, in which local kings struggled for supremacy. Surrounded by opportunities to engage in violence and to pursue earthly ambitions, he was to win a reputation for virtue. The Salamanca manuscript informs us that,

> (S.1) Saint Lasrianus, legate of the Apostolic See and glorious bishop of the church of Lethglen [Leighlin], was by worldly standards, born of most noble ancestors. His father Cairellus was sprung from the higher nobility of the northern part of Ireland, his mother whose name was Gemma was daughter of [A]Edanus, king of Scotiae and niece of the king of Britanniae. He adorned his pedigree, distinguished on both sides, by holy behaviour and good actions.

Laisren's family was of the Ulaid. The Ulaid were a Celtic people who from their stronghold at Emhain Mhacha had once ruled an area which approximated to modern Ulster. Heroic stories of the Ulaid, particularly the famous 'Táin Bó Cuailnge' and its cycle of related sagas about Emhain Mhacha and Cú Chulainn, evolved when the power of the Ulaid was at its height and these stories achieved the status of a national epic in early Irish literature. However, the Ulaid had gradually lost ground to the Uí Neill and others and, by the period of Laisren's birth in the sixth century, they were mainly confined to the north-eastern coastal area from Antrim, through Down, to Louth. Two of the local Ulaid 'septs', or clans, were the Dál Riada and the Dál Fiatach. Laisren's mother was of the former and his father, ostensibly, of the latter.[1]

A mother of Dál Riada

The Dál Riada inhabited Antrim, from where they gradually created a colony across the water, encompassing some of the mainland and islands of modern Scotland. The centre of power of the Dál Riada in Ireland was at Dunseverick, overlooking the sea. The Dál Riada are believed to be those Irish from whom Argyll got its name, 'earr a ghaideal' signifying the 'limit/boundary of the Gaels', and their overseas territory was roughly commensurate with the later counties of Argyll and Bute.[2]

Laisren's grandfather, Aedán mac Gabráin, became the most important king of the overseas Dál Riada. That 'Gabrán' of whom Aedán was a son had himself been known as 'king of Monadh'. In a very old manuscript Laisren's mother is likewise said to be 'of Monadh', which appears to have been an alternative name for an area including at least part of the western highlands and islands of what is now Scotland. Sources, as we shall see, indicate that one of Laisren's uncles was Blaan, reputed abbot of a monastic settlement on the island of Bute in the Firth of Clyde.[3]

A father of Dál Fiatach

For their part, the Dál Fiatach had their centre of power in eastern Co. Down, at Dún-dá-Lethglass, where St Patrick is said to have been buried. This corresponds to the modern Downpatrick. During the sixth century the Dál Fiatach were also busy on naval expeditions in the Irish Sea, from Wales to Scotland. A certain Cairell reigned as their king in the mid-sixth century. He may have been the same 'Cairell' who is said by the author of the Salamanca manuscript to have been Laisren's father and to have been 'sprung from the higher nobility of the northern part of Ireland'. In the book of Ballymote there is a curious verse which suggests that Cairell of Dún-dá-Lethglass was 'victor of Manua'. Praised as the 'diadem of a host', his passing is lamented thus: 'Dead is he, who vanquished Manu, of sorrow at cold Arran'. If this Cairell was indeed Laisren's father then his death at Arran may have influenced Laisren's later decision to go there.[4]

In 572 Cairell was succeeded as king of the Dál Fiatach by one of his sons, Báetán. Some old sources give identical ancestry for both Báetán and Laisren, namely that they were sons of Cairell, son of Muredaig, descendant of Forgo. Thus, these sources strengthen the assumption that Cairell of the Dál Fiatach was in fact Laisren's father. If Báetán was Laisren's brother and if his succession meant that Cairell had died, then the latest possible date at which Laisren can have been born was 573. The accounts of Laisren's life, as we shall see, state that Laisren himself declined an invitation to become the king of his people. Báetán dominated all of the Ulaid during his brief reign from 572 to 581/2. He appears to have ruled the Isle of Man and the Isle of Skye and to have received tribute from far and near. Some Ulster genealogists later described him as 'rí Éren ocus Alban' ('king of Ireland and Scotland'). It is said that even Aedán mac Gabráin was obliged to do Báetán homage at Rinn Seimne (Island Magee near Larne). If Laisren and Báetán were brothers by the same mother then Báetán had obliged his own grandfather, Aedán mac Gabráin, to submit to him. This would not be surprising as there were at the time many complex struggles and alliances. However, it would soon transpire that Aedán and the Dál Riada, not Báetán and the Dál Fiatach, were actually in the ascendant on the Irish Sea.[5]

Irish-Celtic settlement in Britain

Not only the Ulaid but also other Celts from Ireland had invaded Britain following the final withdrawal of Roman forces in the early fifth century. There were Leinster settlements in both north and south Wales and on the Isle of Man. There were regular raids by Irish Celts on western England. It is possible, but not certain, that even before the Dál Riada invasion itself Celts from Ireland had settled in what is now western Scotland. However, the land and isles north of the Firth of Clyde and the Firth of Forth long continued to be ruled by the Picts. South of the Clyde the British Celts remained dominant, those whom Ptolemy identified as the 'Dumnonii' occupying modern Ayrshire and the 'Novantae' living in Galloway. The most eminent king among the British Celts of this area at the close of the Roman period had been Ceredig Gwledig, a person generally identified as the 'Coroticus' who engaged in piratical raids on Ireland and who was accused by (Saint) Patrick of carrying off newly baptised members of his Irish flock. There may also have been a distinct early Irish settlement in the Rinns of Galloway.[6]

The Dál Riada invasion of the western highlands and islands occurred no later than the fifth century and is said to have been spear-headed by a fleet carrying 150 men from Ireland. It has been suggested that these were invited as allies by the British Celts, in order to screen the Clyde area from Inverness and Skye where the Picts ruled. At least one Clyde king gave his son an Irish name and married him to an Irish wife. Old annals record that the Dál Riadan force was led by three sons of Erc. These were Loarn, Aengus and

Fergus. Each brother established his own centre of power. The 'kindred' or people of Loarn occupied the northern part of present-day Argyll and had their seat at Oban, whilst the kindred of Aengus occupied Islay. The descendants of Fergus, known as Cinél Gabrán and whose most famous king was Laisren's grandfather, had Kintyre and Knapdale. Their chief stronghold is thought to have stood on the bare isolated rock of Dunadd, which rises to thirty-three metres in Crinan Moss. A place on Arran, 'Suidhe Fhearghais', is associated with their ancestor. This Fergus is reputed to have been blessed by St Patrick who, we are told, prophesied to him that one of his descendants should occupy the throne of Dál Riada and Fortrenn forever. Fortrenn was the name of a kingdom of the southern Picts. It is said of the Dál Riadans that, 'they brought with them the Gaelic language and the Christian religion'. Controverted legend has it that Fergus also brought from Ireland to Iona that coronation stone of Scottish kings which later became known as the 'Stone of Scone'.[7]

Kingdom of the isles

Dominating as they did the northern of two entrances to the Irish Sea, the Dál Riada were strategically well positioned. Such islands and coasts as came to be ruled by their kings subsequently constituted the bulk of the Norwegian kingdom of the southern isles, as well as the still later domain of the 'lords of the isles' and their allies. Dál Riadan influence extended even to the Isle of Man, which lies in the middle of the Irish Sea and which was long a natural focus in the struggle for maritime power. These places and their inhabitants had a certain collective identity of their own which was gradually lost when most of the territories finally became part of a modern centralised Scotland. Contemplating the Isle of Man, which even yet retains some degree of independence, the historian F. J. Byrne has remarked that,

> The writing of national history as a genre has had the unfortunate result of obscuring entities once important in their own right that have not survived as nation states or even as geographical units.[8]

It was to Laisren's grandfather, Aedán mac Gabráin, that the overseas Dál Riada owed their eventual dominance. As early as 580 Aedán is thought to have led an allied expedition to the Orkneys, which lie far off the northern coast of Scotland. Details of this adventure are sparse and we have already noticed that at that time Aedán was still in the shadow of the Dál Fiatach king, Báetán. However, Báetán died in 581 or 582. About then the king of the southern Picts also passed away. Aedán seized his chance to embark on a long series of expansionist raids on neighbouring territories. Between 574 and 608 he conquered a considerable part of the kingdom of the Picts, perhaps as far as the North Sea. There is some evidence that he possessed Menteith and he is said to have presented St Berach with a fort at Aberfoyle. He was victorious in a battle at 'Manu'. Welsh manuscripts suggest that he undertook an expedition to Strathclyde, with a possible battle in Galloway. A poem refers to Aedán as 'king of the Forth'. It may have been from the latter area that he eventually attacked Northumbria, a step too far which was to lead in 603 to his forces suffering a signal defeat at the hands of Aethelfrith.[9]

Clearly, the Dál Riada under Aedán had a wide sphere of influence. Archibald Duncan, the Scottish historian, has described Laisren's grandfather as 'a tough opportunist, enemy of all his neighbours and master of most of them'. Yet, notwithstanding the apparently fierce nature of contemporary confrontations between small kingdoms, personal relationships were established which sometimes led to marriage. One source suggests that Aedán's own mother, Laisren's great-grandmother, was a British Celt. Duncan thinks that Aedán himself may have married a Pictish princess, although he is said to have fought the Picts continuously for thirteen years. By some woman, or women, Aedán is reported to have fathered at least seven sons, many of whom died in battle. His daughter who became Laisren's mother was called 'Gemma', which is a Latinised name suggesting Roman-British influence. One of Aedán's own sons or grandsons bore the British name, Artúr, which appears to have been rare at that time.[10]

Aedán and Colum Cille

The circumstances in which Aedán was made king and consolidated his position were themselves remarkable and certainly reflect complex political inter-relationships between the various Celtic and Pictish kingdoms. Deeply involved in these was Criomhthann, better known as Colum Cille (literally 'dove of the church') or Columba. A member of the northern Uí Neill, Colum Cille was highly respected in his own lifetime and has been described as 'the pioneer of the Irish *peregrinatio* [wandering overseas] and the first saint of impeccably royal blood'. It was he who on Iona was to consecrate Aedán as king of Dál Riada and it helps to understand the context in which Laisren lived if one briefly considers certain events in the life of Colum Cille.[11]

During the twenty years before he left Ireland for Iona, Colum Cille had established many monasteries. Why exactly he departed for his new island home is a mystery but his move appears to have been connected with an assembly at which he was condemned or even excommunicated for some unknown offence. The chief account of his life was written within a century of his death, by Adomnán (Adamnan), his later successor as abbot of Iona from 679 to 704. Adomnán does not suggest that Colum Cille left Ireland as a penance for his purported involvement in a contemporary battle. That popular tale was a later embellishment. Also, contrary to popular belief, Colum Cille subsequently returned from Iona to visit Ireland on a number of occasions.[12]

The island of Iona lay in the watery reaches between the territories of the Picts to the north and those of the Dál Riada to the south. However, we simply do not know if Colum Cille sought the permission of either or even both peoples before he settled there. He is believed to have played a crucial part in the conversion to Christianity of the Pictish king and some of that king's followers but he and his monks did not embark on widespread missionary work among the Picts, as is sometimes thought. When missionary work was later undertaken by the monks of Iona it was principally directed further south in Britain. Colum Cille gained a reputation for diplomacy in his dealings with the Picts and he seems to have deployed the same skills in connection with Dál Riada. The suspicion arises in this context that he did not forget the political interests of the northern Uí Neill, from whose royal family he sprang and in connection with whom his actions may have led to his leaving Ireland for Iona.[13]

Colum Cille arrived at Iona in 563, a decade before Laisren's grandfather became king. It seems that, at first, the relationship between the two men was not good. Thus,

> in the commentary to the Bodleian *Amra Choluimb Chille*, we find Aedán determined to prove Colum Cille a liar and a fool. But Colum Cille, who is described here as Aedán's *anmchara* or spiritual director, is too clever for him. One of the tests involved Aedán's daughter, Conchenn [presumably Gemma's sister or half-sister]. Again, [in the same text], forty-seven druids are summoned by Aedán to curse the saint. They are, of course, defeated.[14]

Colum Cille was not easily persuaded that Aedán should become king of Dál Riada. Adomnán writes that it required divine intervention for the saint to make his ultimate decision. He was on the island of Hinba, in some kind of trance, when an angel appeared bearing a glass book on the ordination of kings:

> But when he refused to ordain Aedán as king, according to what was commanded him in the book, because he loved Iógenán, Aedán's brother more, the angel suddenly stretched out his hand and struck the holy man with a scourge, the livid scar from which remained on his side all the days of his life. And the angel addressed these words, saying: 'Know surely that I am sent to you by God, with the book of glass, in order that, according to what you have read in it, you shall ordain Aedán to the kingship. But if you refuse to obey the command, I shall strike you again'.

Only when the angel had appeared three nights in a row to repeat his command did the holy man submit. Then Colum Cille sailed over to Iona and ordained Aedán, who arrived about the same time. He also blessed him. Adomnán adds that, among the words of the ordination, Colum Cille prophesied future things of Aedán's sons, grand-sons and great-grandsons. But Adomnán does not identify Aedán's grandsons or give details of these prophesies, so we do not learn if one referred specifically to Laisren. On another occasion Colum Cille prophesied that certain of Aedán's sons would be killed. A later biographer, Cumméne, added that Colum Cille also warned Aedán and his descendants not to do evil 'to me or to my kindred who are in Ireland', an admonition which indicates that Colum Cille was still actively interested in the welfare of the northern Uí Neill.[15]

Given Aedán's subsequent reputation as a ferocious warrior, sceptics may suspect that the story of the angel was invented to dress up some nastier and worldly form of compulsion. In any event, Colum Cille's endorsement of Aedán is highly significant as the first recorded Christian ordination of a Gaelic king and, whatever the earlier relationship between the two men, Colum Cille and Aedán soon became allies and even friends:

> It was undoubtedly their joint statesmanship which guided the destiny of this little Irish-speaking colony in Argyll until it amalgamated ultimately with the Pictish kingdom... Already in 628 the Irish annals speak of his [Aedán's] son and successor, Eochaid Buide, as *rex Pictorum* [king of the Picts].[16]

Poets and priests

In 575, Colum Cille and Aedán attended the convention of Druim Cett, which was principally concerned with the relationship between the Dál Riada in Ireland and their neighbours on land and sea. The convention overall appears to have constituted an alliance between the Dál Riada and the northern Uí Neill at the expense of the Dál Fiatach. Colum Cille, himself a northern Uí Neill, is said to have prophetically warned Aedán against breaking this alliance and one of Aedán's grandsons was later perceived to have brought disaster on Dál Riada by doing just that. Thus, in 637 the Dál Riada were to be permanently weakened by their defeat in the battle at Mag Roth (Moyra, Co. Down).[17]

Legend has it that the convention of Druim Cett also decided against the expulsion of the 'filí' or 'poets' from Ireland. These stood accused of avarice, idleness, exactions and insolence but Colum Cille is said to have spoken up for them, recommending reform rather than the destruction of their order.[18]

That there were undoubtedly strains between these poets and early Christians is a matter worth considering because of its relevance to events in the later life of Laisren. It should be borne in mind that the professional 'poets' of Ireland were what one writer has called a 'protective metamorphosis' of the old Druidic order. People feared the force of their words. They not only celebrated the deeds of warriors, recited genealogies and chanted dirges for the dead. Their opposition could undermine an individual's social standing and their 'satires' or maledictions were even considered capable of causing physical injury or death. In a society with few written records, as was Ireland in the sixth century, these men effectively controlled access to and interpretation of past events. 'Their power', says the historian James Carney, 'was thus somewhat analogous to the power of the church' and the story of Colum Cille's intervention on their behalf may be interpreted as an attempted compromise between the old and new orders. By the seventh century the 'filí' had become virtually the sole inheritors of such Druidic functions and privileges as survived and were not only poets but seers, teachers, advisers of rulers and witnesses of contracts.[19]

The Scoti

Colum Cille has been described as 'undoubtedly the great man in the expansion of Dál Riada during the sixth century'. The influence of the alliance between him and Aedán was considerable and lasting. Their religion and language were to inform the culture of modern Scotland. Gaelic became for long the principal tongue of the Scottish people. Irish monks established various monasteries, including one on Lindisfarne, that other 'Holy Island', which lies in the North Sea off Northumbria, and they revived Christianity in post-Roman Britain. Indeed, it is to the invading Dál Riada that modern Scotland owes its very name. The Irish who came to Argyll and the western isles had been known previously as 'Scoti' or 'Scotti' and that designation was gradually transferred with them across the water during the process of colonisation. Even after their defeat at Mag Roth in 637, the kings of Dál Riada continued to be a formidable force. The kingdom of the southern Picts, with its seat at Scone, was eventually merged with that of Dál Riada and became known as Atholl, which is said to derive from Ath-Fótla, 'Second Ireland' or 'New Ireland'. The union of Picts and Scots was completed under the Dál Riadan king, Kenneth MacAlpin, who died in 858. The standard lists of Scottish kings give a clear line of descent from Laisren's great-grandfather to Kenneth's son.[20]

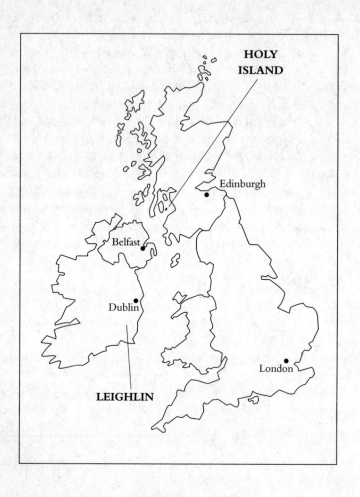

HOLY
ISLAND

Edinburgh

Belfast

Dublin

LEIGHLIN

London

CHAPTER 2

Miracle-worker and monk

L AISREN WAS almost certainly born on the island of Ireland itself, although this detail is merely implicit in the accounts of his life. The Salamanca manuscript indicates that, from a very early age, Laisren was regarded as a special person:

(S.2) Certain signs at his birth gave promise of the extraordinary holiness of this man. The midwife, instructed from above, taking the child just born to her bosom, made the sign of the cross over her sterile womb with his hand, and became capable of bearing children. A certain man named Senachus who was blind from birth instantly got the power of sight after washing his eyes with the water in which the child had been bathed.

After this his mother [Gemma] returned to her native land with the child where he stayed for seven years and shone with miracles. There, to the great amazement of those who witnessed it, he saved his nurse from the region of death after she had been bitten by a snake. As soon as he made the sign of the saving cross on the wounded hand the whole poisoned swelling disappeared.

When the author of the Salamanca manuscript writes that Gemma 'returned to her native land' after Laisren's birth, what land is denoted? Her father was 'King of Scotiae' (S.1). The Fitzsimon text specifies that Gemma's 'native land' was 'Alba', a name used in the later middle ages for parts of modern Scotland. An older source than Fitzsimon, as we saw earlier, refers to Laisren's mother being 'of Monadh', which was a designation for areas of the western highlands and isles. From this we deduce that Laisren was born in Ireland and then taken to the territory of the overseas Dál Riada.

Gemma's return with Laisren to 'her native land' may have followed his father's death. Indeed, if the convention of Druim Cett was a Dál Riadan alliance at the expense of the Dál Fiatach, as is believed by modern scholars, it possibly led to tensions between the families of Laisren's parents. In any event, thereafter, he is said by his biographer to have remained in his mother's land for seven years. Some of his time in Gemma's 'native land' was possibly passed at the Dál Riadan stronghold of Dunadd, where his grandfather could look after his interests, and some of it may have been spent on Bute, where his reputed uncle's monastery stood across from Arran. He may even have met Colum Cille, who was living nearby on Iona until 597. Perhaps Laisren was actually named in honour of Laisren of Inishmurray, a saint also known as 'Molaise', who is said by some writers to have been Colum Cille's spiritual guide or 'anam chara' ('soul-friend') and who is thought to have been involved in the latter's decision to leave Ireland. Given Colum Cille's close relationship with Aedán mac Gabráin, one may reasonably speculate that the former was instrumental in naming the latter's grandson.[1]

Uncle Blaan of Bute

As Laisren's fame spread, his 'uncle' Blaan of Bute desired to see the child. Bute lies in the Firth of Clyde and Blaan is associated there with the old monastic site of Kingarth, which faces Arran and Holy Island. The islands of Bute, Arran and Islay were bracketed together in Irish literature and it has been suggested that the history of Arran until the thirteenth century is nearly the same as that of Bute. Blaan, a bishop, was later adopted as the patron saint of the Scottish town of Dunblane.[2]

While on his visit to Laisren, we are told, the bishop's horse was stolen by a thief:

> (S.3) The reverend pontiff Blaanus, the child's uncle, hearing that he shone with miracles, set out to visit him. While he was being joyfully received by the child's guardians, one of his team of horses was stolen away. Hearing this, the bishop as if making a sign to rouse the boy, said, 'He whom we are visiting should either get back our horse or untie another'.

According to the Fitzsimon manuscript Blaan said this in jest. However, as the Salamanca manuscript indicates above, the words were a means of awakening a potential power within his nephew:

(S.3 continued) But God from on high heard the wish of His disciple and made the thief return to them with the horse. When the bishop asked the reason for his return, the thief answered, 'The soldiers of King Cairellus are following me, so I take refuge under the protection of his son'. Those who were there and heard this went out to see the sight but saw nobody following hím. Seeing this wonder, the bishop gave thanks to God and went back to his own affairs.

(S.4) After this his mother, being warned in a vision and instructed by an angel, returned to his own country and gave him to holy Mundus to be educated.

Fitzsimon (F.2, F.4) gives the latter's name as 'Munnus'. This 'Mundus' or 'Munnus' was perhaps the saint who is associated with the beautiful isle of St Munde in Loch Leven and who was sometime abbot of Kilmund in Argyll and who, apparently, is also thought to be one and the same as 'Fintan Munnu' of Bangor, whom the community of Iona despatched to Leinster to found a monastery there in fulfilment of a prophecy by Colum Cille. Remarkable for his leprosy, as we shall see, Fintan Munnu is said to have later disagreed cordially with Laisren on a matter of considerable importance to the contemporary church.[3]

A young student

Laisren, as we have seen from the Salamanca manuscript, is said to have been brought out of the land of his birth for seven years before returning 'to his own country' to be educated by this 'holy Mundus'. However, both Arthur and Fitzsimon give just 'four' years as the period spent in his mother's 'native land'. Thus, on the face of it, Laisren was not much older than either four or seven when he was placed in a monastery under 'Mundus' or 'Munnus'. Perhaps this is to read the text too literally. Yet, it is said of another Irish saint of the period that, 'when he [Barra, or Finbar of Cork] was seven years old, three clerics got permission to take him with them to study in Leinster'.[4] Barra, as we shall see, is said to have been friendly later with Laisren.

It was long common for wealthy Irish families to foster their own children to poorer folk at an early age and in modern times children have been sent to boarding schools as young as five or six. However, Fitzsimon's editors appear unwilling to accept that a child so young would have been taken into a monastery and they suggest that Laisren must have left for 'Alba' at the age of twelve or fourteen. They have even included in a footnote their convenient deduction, based on assumption rather than any evidence, that he must have been born around the year 566! This would have made Laisren about thirty years old when, as is written, he later set off for Rome and was there ordained.

In any event, the young Laisren is said to have been duly educated by 'holy Mundus' and,

> (S.4 continued) Having been taught by his wisdom and formed by the example of his life, he worked extraordinary miracles. On a certain day, when they were both milling and there was not sufficient flow of water in the place, on the instructions of his master he went out with his rod and dug up a sod there, where much water leaped up and flowed abundantly for milling.

The Arthur and Fitzsimon versions add that the monastic community, with all God's servants, thereupon rejoiced. The monks recalled the words of Psalm xlv, 5, which proclaim that, 'The stream of the river maketh the city of God joyful'.

> (S.5) At another time when the brothers knew in advance of the coming of pirates, they were in the chapel asking God that they might be safe from the attack of their enemies. When dawn gave an end to night, there were the cruel robbers who having entered the district were now filling the field surrounding the monastery. But as he prayed with the others, they retreated as if from the face of attackers, and abandoning their boat, fled like madmen to their ships.
>
> (S.6) Also at another time, when he took some travellers under his care, there came some dreadful robbers, who neither fearing God nor honouring His servant, cruelly stripped them of everything. But God took vengeance on the enemies of His people. For as soon as they divided the loot, fighting among themselves, they killed one another — and those who with the holy man were rejoicing and praising God in his saint, came to their desired destination with their enemies' loot as well as their own goods.

'Peregrinatio'

When Laisren approached manhood, it is said, his people sought him out as their leader. He declined to accept the position:

> (S.7) All the people of each district in his region wanted holy Lasrianus to be king. But He who once rejected the kingdom of the Jews, gave him the courage to despise power of this kind. So fleeing the face of earthly honour, he sought out an island between Britannia and Scotia, where leading the life of a hermit, he shone with many signs of miracles. He settled there with the intention of eventually travelling and reaching the apostolic threshold to see the relics of the saints.

Where this manuscript gives '*inter Britanniam et Scociam*', Arthur has merely '*inter Britanniam*', while Fitzsimon gives '*inter Britanniam & Albaniam*'. There is no manuscript which identifies the island which Laisren sought out 'between Britannia and Scotia' but local tradition firmly associates him with a small isle just off the east coast of the larger island of Arran, in the Firth of Clyde. This did indeed lie between territory controlled by British Celts, namely the modern Ayr, Dumfries and Galloway of south-west Scotland, and territory of the 'Scoti' or Dál Riadan people who controlled Kintyre, Knapdale, Islay, Argyll and the adjacent districts. The isle on which he is believed to have led the life of a hermit was to be long known as 'Molaise's Island,' before later becoming simply 'The Holy Isle' and 'Holy Island'. He gave his name to the adjacent bay and village of Lam[o]lash. This Scottish holy island must be distinguished from that English Holy Island which lies in the North Sea and which is associated with Cuthbert.

Even before he went to Arran, Laisren envisaged a subsequent journey to Rome. The Salamanca manuscript makes this clear when it states that he had 'the intention of eventually travelling and reaching the apostolic threshold to see the relics of the saints' (S.7). Yet he wished first to pass part of his life in relative solitude. He thus became a hermit or 'anchorite'.

Such a retreat as Laisren now embarked upon was one feature of that practice of withdrawal from one's homeland known in the early church as '*peregrinatio*', a Latin term which signifies journeying. Another feature was a pilgrimage to some famous shrine such as the tombs of the apostles in Rome. Many who left Ireland on their personal *peregrinatio* did not return but founded religious settlements in other lands. These men often had a high social background. Others stayed closer to home. The promontories and islands around Ireland and Scotland came to be dotted with 'cells' to which, in the words of Colum Cille's biographer, men retreated 'seeking the place of one's resurrection'. They took inspiration from stories of 'the desert fathers' of Egypt and of the middle-east, especially from that of St Anthony by Athanasius. At Iona and on some other islands there was provision for such a withdrawal to occur even within the vicinity of the community and the early Irish 'Rule of the Anchorites', known as the 'Rule of Colum Cille', enjoins on the anchorite to be 'alone in a desert place apart in the neighbourhood of a chief monastery if you distrust in your conscience to be in the company of many'. Thus, anchoritism was considered an intrinsic part of the monastic rule rather than a reaction against it. One leading church historian writes that, 'the religious graduated to the life of the anchorite as a result of a period of preparation within the community', and that, 'the anchorite life in the Celtic church was looked upon as a degree to which only the more advanced monks might attain'.[5]

To what extent Laisren saw himself in the mainstream of *peregrinatio* or anchoritism we cannot say. His hermitage on Holy Island was, presumably, under the physical protection of Dál Riadan forces. His uncle Blaan's foundation at Kingarth on Bute was just a short journey away by sea. Did it become Laisren's 'chief monastery' for a period? Or did Colum Cille himself take a personal interest in Aedán's grandson? We do not know.

There was another dimension to the choice of islands as hermitages. From at least the time of Homer the Celtic peoples, including those of Gaul, were linked by a tradition of sacred islands off the Atlantic coasts of Britain and Ireland, — 'links which also remind us of earlier Greek stories of the "islands of the blest" west of the Pillars of Hercules, and the magic island of Circe in the western seas'.[6] One particular island which was regarded as special by the ancient Irish was Arran, to which Laisren was now bound.

Arran

Lying off the coast of Ayrshire in the Firth of Clyde, the island of Arran is passed to the east by ships making their way in and out of the port of Glasgow. The island is about nineteen miles long and up to ten miles wide and was rich in history long before Laisren set eyes on it. Its earlier inhabitants have left us a pre-historic legacy in stone which is of great archaeological value.[7]

The earliest literary references to Arran appear in medieval Gaelic manuscripts. In these Arran was sometimes identified with the supernatural island of Emhain Abhlach, or 'Emhain of the Apple-Trees', a beautiful wooded realm associated with Manannán mac Lir, god of the sea. His mythical home was on the Isle of Man, located centrally for the sea-faring Celts, and elsewhere Man itself is identified as Emhain Abhlach. The name 'Emhain Abhlach' is echoed in that of the Avalon of British Celtic myth which was adopted into Arthurian literature. Sources also indicate that the islands of Arran, Islay, Aran (off Galway), Rathlin and Man had defined the outer reaches of Ireland for its earliest Celtic inhabitants and it was to these islands that their defeated predecessors, the Fir Bolg, were said to have retreated. They lived there amongst their 'under [water-] phantoms' or 'Fomoiri', whose leader was Balar of the one eye.[8]

Arran, like much of Western Scotland, is also steeped in the ancient folklore of the Fianna and their leader, Fionn. The Fianna were a mythical warrior-class which the Irish Celts regarded as semi-divine. Arran was fondly regarded as a playground of the Fianna by the people of Gaelic Ireland, in whose ambit of cultural influence the island lay for at least a millennium. One celebrated manuscript, which survives from the twelfth century, recounts how St Patrick supposedly met with two remnants of the ancient Fianna, namely Oisín and Caeilte. In his 'colloquy with the ancients', Patrick discussed many things, including Arran:

'It is well Caeilte: what was the best hunting that the Fianna ever had, whether in Ireland or in Scotland (Alba)?' 'The hunting of Arran'. Patrick enquired: 'Where is that land?' 'Betwixt Scotland and Pictland [idir Albain ocus Cruithentua[i]th]: on the first day of the trogan-month (which is now called lughnasadh i.e. Lammas-tide) we, to the number of the Fianna's three battalions, practised to repair thither and there have our fill of hunting until such time as from the tree tops the cuckoo would call in Ireland. More melodious than all the music whatsoever it was to give ear to the voices of the birds as they rose from the billows and from the island's coast line, thrice fifty separate flocks there were that encircled her, and they clad in grey brilliance of all colours: as blue, and green, and azure, and yellow'. Here Caeilte uttered a lay [poem/song].[9]

The description of Arran as lying between (idir) 'Albain ocus Cruithentua[i]th' is in keeping with the language of the accounts of the life of Laisren which do not refer specifically to his going either to Arran or to Holy Island but, vaguely, to an unnamed island 'between Britannia and

Scotia (*inter Britanniam et Scociam*)' (S.7) and '*inter Britanniam & Albaniam*' (F.6).[10] The Fianna lay which Caeilte proceeded to utter has been translated poetically by Kuno Meyer from the twelfth century manuscript. It begins,

> Arran of the many stags,
> The sea strikes against its shoulder,
> Isle where companies are fed,
> Ridge on which blue spears are reddened.
>
> Skittish deer are on her peaks,
> Delicious berries on her manes,
> Cool water in her rivers,
> Mast [fruit] upon her dun oaks.[11]

Macrie Moor on Arran has been described as 'a surviving Bronze Age landscape of outstanding importance, still largely covered by peat'. Here are cairns, standing stones and hut circles. Some of the remains date to before 3000 BC and the area appears to have been much used for ceremonial and farming purposes. The moor stretches back from the west coast of Arran, just north of Shiskine and the iron age fort on Drumadoon headland. Along this coast are caves of historic significance, including one associated with Fionn. The stones on Macrie Moor stand as high as eighteen feet and are a favourite resort of visitors to the island.[12]

On Macrie Moor certain distinctive stones were known as Fionn's 'judgement stone' and as Fionn's 'cauldron seat', where he was said to have placed his cooking pot! Near Macrie Moor rises Ard Bheinn, where there is a cave long associated with the supernatural. This hill and others by it were marked on a Victorian map of Arran as 'the Fairy Hills'.[13] On their south side a path ran across Arran and this path, as we shall see, is thought to have been walked by medieval pilgrims. It led from near Fionn's 'judgement stone' through Clauchan, the place where Laisren is reputed to be buried, over to Lamlash Bay. Thence pilgrims might embark by boat to inspect a 'judgement stone' which is associated with Laisren and which will be considered below. By Lamlash Bay stood a remarkable monument, said to include a number of cromlechs. Many Arran mounds were thought to be the graves of Fionn's heroes and one in particular, which was associated with Diarmaid and his dog, was said to have been revered until the eighteenth century by people who travelled to Arran from Argyll and who went around it on their knees.[14]

The fort of Fionn, Dún Fionn or Dunfinn, stands 'on a round eminence of considerable elevation near the point of Clachlands', which is that promontory which shelters Lamlash Bay to the north. This may be the 'Dún Finn' of 'Alba' which features in the Irish dirge, 'The Death of the sons of Uisneach'.[15]

The hero Fionn and Laisren's grandfather are connected by one of the most extraordinary stories in Irish 'history'. This story collapses the distinctions between mythology and verifiable fact so that the sea-god Manannán, Fionn and Aedán Mac Gabráin are joined in a triangular relationship. The tale has often been discussed by scholars. It tells how Fiachna was king of the Dál nAraidhe, the third of the three leading Ulaid septs in north-east Ireland. He went overseas to help Aedán Mac Gabráin, Laisren's grandfather. In his absence Manannán mac Lir appeared in the guise of a nobleman to Fiachna's wife and told her that unless she consented to bear his son then her husband would die in battle next day. She consented. The next day Manannán, in the same noble guise, appeared at the head of the armies of Aedán and Fiachna and vanquished their enemies. The son who is said to have been born of this union was Mongán, the historical king who died in 615. When the child was three nights old Manannán supposedly came and took him away to the Land of Promise where he was fostered until he was twelve or sixteen years old. One account suggests that Mongán was Fionn reborn, a version which expresses a traditional Irish belief in rebirth. The folklorist Daithi O hOgain is in no doubt that legends about Fionn were readily grafted by poets onto the person of Mongán.[16]

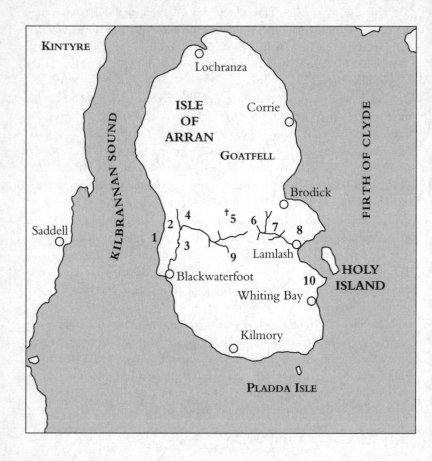

1. King's (or Fionn's) Cave
2. Macrie Moor
3. St Molios Church, Shiskine
4. Clauchan Glen
5. Cnoc na Croise (Hill of the Cross)
6. Lag na Croise (Hollow of the Cross)
7. Benlister Glen
8. Kilbride Church
9. Cnoc na Dáil (Hill of Gatherings)
10. Kingscross Point

Clauchan Water flows west.

Benlister Burn flows east.

CHAPTER 3

The Holy Isle

L AISREN IS unlikely to have been the first Christian to make his way to Arran. However, little is known about the initial impact of Christianity on the island or about the circumstances in which its earliest churches, long since ruinous or destroyed, were built. They honoured Patrick (Kilpatrick), Brighid (Kilbride), Donnan (Kildonan), Mary (Kilmorie) and Michael (Kilmichael). Tales about Patrick have him welcomed by Erc's sons in Dál Riada and are on a par with very many others which place Patrick all over Ireland. Kilpatrick, from where one can clearly see the coast of Antrim, was reputed to be a burial place for people from Ireland.[1]

Associations between Colum Cille and Arran are not strong. 'Suidhe Chalum Chille', by 'The String' road, is said to be where he rested when crossing the island and near it a holy well also bears his name. However, one Scottish church historian has noted that throughout the former territories of Dál Riada about thirty old churches are said to have been dedicated to Colum Cille, 'the great majority in the islands' and at least one on Kintyre.[2]

There is no evidence that Colum Cille took any interest in Laisren's education or in his presence on Holy Island. Yet the Salamanca manuscript states that when Laisren later left his hermitage he did so to go to Rome, 'at the request of Columba and other holy men' (S.7). Whatever the truth of that assertion, it seems somewhat unlikely that the king of Dál Riada's grandson, while living in the Firth of Clyde, would not have met the king's great adviser who was over on Iona.

In sight of Ireland

That 'holy isle' which is associated with Laisren lies in Lamlash Bay on the east coast of Arran and shelters a great natural harbour which has served many vessels and fleets, including very often those of the Vikings and of the Royal Navy. One visitor who admired the area during the late eighteenth century was Thomas Pennant, (only afterwards did Brodick come to supplant Lamlash as the first port of call of travellers to Arran):

> In the afternoon leave Brodick Castle, descend by the village of Kilbride, and reach the harbour of Lamlash, where our vessel lay at anchor in the safest port in the universe; a port perfectly Virgillian.

> *Hic insula portum*
> *Efficit objectu laterum.*

> A beautiful semicircular bay forms one part: while the lofty island of Lamlash extending before the mouth secures it from the east winds: leaving on each side a safe and easy entrance. The whole circumference is about nine miles; and the depth of the water is sufficient for the largest ships.[3]

Although Holy Island is just two miles long, it can take four hours to circumambulate it at a comfortable pace. There is no easy track on the eastern side and walking on the boulders and stones is quite demanding. Rising high above the walker is the central peak of Mullach Mór. The island on which Laisren made his hermitage may be small but it is striking:

> Holy Isle is a wild, heather-covered rock, a volcanic upthrust, two miles long and 1,030 feet high. From every angle it has a different shape. From the village of Lamlash [on Arran] it is long and symmetrical, with two rounded peaks, cleft by a deep gully. In the summer, when a full moon rises between them, Lamlash Bay is one of the loveliest places on earth. People at Whiting Bay see it as a crouching lion, guarding over the Firth, and from the Corrie shore it is round at the base with one steep point. To mariners passing on the Firth of Clyde [to Glasgow] it appears to be a rocky foreland of the mainland of Arran, so completely does it fill the entrances to the bay.[4]

From Holy Island one may view Arran, Bute, Kintyre and the Scottish mainland. It is said to be possible in very clear weather to see Ireland from its steep and somewhat dangerous peak of Mullach Mór. Ireland, thirty-five miles distant, is certainly visible from the west coast of Arran. Faint folk memories were all that remained into the modern period of the sea-journeys west which had once been common when Arran lay for a millennium in the Irish sphere of influence. In 1895 a story was told in Gaelic by an old crofter living on Arran. It was the implausible tale of a man called Macuga (Cook?)

who accompanies 'na sifri' (the 'fairies' or spirits) on a trip across the sea to Ireland, flying on ragworth. As Macuga prepares to depart one of his good companions calls out some lines. These were perhaps an ancient charm or prayer on the lips of generations of travellers:

Mo righ air mo cheann	My king at my head
Dol thairis am dheann,	Going across in my haste,
Air chirean ran tonn,	On the crests of the waves,
A dh' Eirinn.	To Ireland.[5]

Molaise's cave

The saint's cell, a large overhang of rock over dry ground, is marked on survey maps as 'St Molio's Cave', 'Molio(s)' being now a local variant of Laisren's name. The cave is about half-way along the island, and a little above the shoreline under Mullach Mór. Elsewhere in Scotland a number of other caves were also used as hermitages, including one associated with Colum Cille in Argyllshire.[6]

From just below it on the shore 'St Molio's Cave' appears as a narrow slit in the hillside. It is indeed quite shallow and restricted in size but it is positively roomy by comparison with some of the beehive huts in which Celtic hermits once lived. A latter day monk has explained that, 'the floor of the cave is so low...that anyone sitting inside could not see land or sea but only a vast expanse of sky or clouds, which makes it a prized meditation spot'. The cave faces west by south-west and on a fine evening the sky glows red until a late hour. Kerr-Hunter thought that, 'it could not have been very comfortable in winter when a swirling sou'wester was piping up the Bay'. Perhaps for this reason and for privacy, much of the opening on the outside of the overhang was closed up by a wall, of which some part remains, thereby creating a 'cell'.[7]

In 1807 Headrick visited the place:

I saw a cave on the western side of the island in which he [Molaise] lived. It is an excavation of the red sandstone which forms the basis of the island, formed by the sea when it occupied a higher level than it now does; aided apparently by art. There is a narrow projection of rock, a little elevated above the floor, which is said to have been his bed, and the mouth of the cave seems to have been defended by a wall of loose stones.[8]

In 1263 at Lamlash Bay there gathered a fleet of 150 ships under the command of Haakon, king of the Vikings, who was attempting unsuccessfully to retain Scandinavian influence in western Scotland. A Norwegian chronicler of this event refers to Holy Island as Malas-isle [Malassey]. After a decisive defeat at and near Largs, Haakon returned to Lamlash Bay where he was visited by a deputation of Irishmen intent on enticing him to come to Ireland as an ally in their fight against the Anglo-Normans. The Irish failed to persuade his war-weary force to join them. Before he left the area, Vigleikr, the king's marshal, cut his initials into the roof of Molaise's cave. He was not the first of his countrymen to do so. Seven similar runic inscriptions have been found in the cave and are thought to date from the eleventh century onwards.[9]

In 1908 J. A. Balfour conducted the first archaeological survey of Holy Island. He turned his attention to Molaise's cave which he found silted up with soil almost level to the approach. He removed this, leaving it piled outside in front of the mouth of the cave where it became overgrown. The excavations disclosed steps which led down into the paved part of the interior. The cell was measured and found to be 38.5 feet long by 13 feet at the widest part, which is close to the foot of the steps:

> The cell is paved from the middle of the north-east corner, or for about 26 feet. In this paving is set a large stone raised but little above the paving; it measures 5 feet 11 inches in length by 1 foot 8 inches in depth; the ends lie almost north and south [the so-called 'altar' stone]. Some of the paving having got shifted, an examination was made of the rock below and a drain was found cut out of the solid rock; it passes out under the flags at the foot of the stair.

At the south-west end of the cell there were dug up considerable quantities of shells, mostly of limpet and oyster, as well as the bones of domesticated animals, including mostly young ox, sheep, pig and deer. Also found was what Balfour took to be a fireplace, which had been covered by a soil-slip from outside:

> The fireplace is built with a portion going under the south wall; attached to the wall had been uprights, with a flat stone on the top; unfortunately, the weight of earth above had caused this portion of the fireplace to collapse. The vent is made between the courses of stone forming the wall.

Balfour noted scores of crosses which had been 'made by pilgrims' on the roof and walls of the cave. Some of these are still visible on the rock. He commented upon the runic inscriptions, to which reference was made above in the context of the Norwegian domination of the western isles. He found also that, 'too often has the modern penknife been employed, in vulgar ignorance, to cut initials detrimental to the older relics of pious visitors'. Balfour did not remark upon a particularly fine cross, of some vintage and art, which is found on the outside of the cave above the stair.[10]

Water and rock

Quite near Molaise's cave, and to the south, a crystal-clear spring bubbles out of the hillside. As recently as 1959 this spring, which over the years has become associated locally with Molaise's memory, was thought 'to bring a blessing to those who drink from it' and to heal the ill and it is still venerated even today. Laisren from time to time possibly stood barefoot in the spring or waded up to his waist in the cold sea nearby, while reciting from memory the entire Book of Psalms, — the '150' or 'three fifties' as it was known because of the total number of psalms. Such a penitential practice was regarded as exemplary by anchorites and is quite compatible with the behaviour of Laisren as described by the author of the 'Life of Maignenn' and considered below.[11]

Between the cave and the spring sits a huge block of stone, about seven feet high. The top of the rock has been levelled and what appear to be steps, four seats, a foothold and a hand-grip have been cut into its sides. Incised on the north-east face is an old cross with a ring top. During the past two centuries this boulder has been called the 'Judgement Stone', 'Pulpit Rock', '(Saint's) Table' or 'Saint's Chair', but it is not clear what purpose it ever served. Its common names recall those of other stones near Macrie on Arran which were long associated with Fionn and which were known popularly as the 'Panel's', 'Trial' or 'Judgement' Stone[s] or Fionn's 'cauldron seat'. At Auchencairn a great 'rock of the fire' was used prior to 1800 for preaching purposes. Scottish Presbyterians made some penitents sit on an elevated 'cutty stool'. Perhaps Laisren's boulder once served as a place for preaching, pronouncing judgement and doing penance.[12]

A mysterious stone

Lying in front of Molaise's 'Judgement Stone', towards the sea, is a hollowed stone with a circular depression. Presumably it is the same stone which writers such as Balfour have thought to have once served as a font for 'holy water'. In 1908 Balfour wrote that this 'rudely chiselled stone...suffered some injury about two years ago by some vandals removing it and throwing it upon the rocky shore, from which it is separated only by a narrow path; it is now carefully restored to its original position'. Yet according to one visitor the alleged font, 'a shapeless slab with a depression probably caused by sea action...is unconvincing as an antiquity'. Balfour was more impressed,

> We venture to think that the primitive cell, the 'Judgement Stone', the holy water font, and the well, form, in their conjunction, as interesting a group associated with the name of an early saint as exists in Scotland.[13]

If the circular depression served any purpose, and it seems to this author to have been worked by hand, was it sometimes a receptacle for that special rounded and portable stone which was traditionally connected with the saint? This was long used for swearing oaths, a fact which may be relevant to why the adjacent big rock has been known as the 'Judgement Stone'. The portable stone, sacred to the memory of Molaise, was associated also with healing and warfare. About 1695 it was described as,

> a valuable curiosity on this isle [of Arran], which they call Baul Muluy, i.e. Molingus his stone globe; this saint was chaplain to Mack Donald of the isles; his name is celebrated here on the account of this globe, so much esteemed by the inhabitants. This stone for its intrinsic value has been carefully transmitted to posterity for several ages. It is a green stone much like a globe in figure, about the bigness of a goose-egg. The virtues of it is to remove stitches from the sides of sick persons, by laying it close to the place affected, and if the patient does not outlive the distemper, they say the stone removes out of the bed of its own accord, and *e contra*. The natives use the stone for swearing decisive oaths upon it.[14]

This tells us something about how the stone was regarded around 1695, although it is clear that Molaise cannot have been, in the usual sense, 'chaplain' to a MacDonald who lived long after him. MacDonald of the isles is said to have carried the stone to battle and the writer here adds a statement which is reminiscent of how Laisren's powers were reputedly instrumental in routing pirates in Ireland. He notes that the people of Arran believed that enemies ran away whenever this stone was thrown in front of them.

The 'Baul Muluy' was clearly as fearsome as the mythical sling-shot of Lugh but it was not unique. Inishmurray, Co. Sligo, for example, is home to two peculiar round stones which fit into other hollowed stones and which are known as the 'speckled' or 'cursing' stones. The custody of Molaise's stone on Arran was the special responsibility of a family called the 'Clan-Chattons', alias 'Mack Intosh', of 'Baellmianich', who were once followers of MacDonald. It was kept wrapped in a linen cloth, around which was a woollen cloth, and it was locked in a chest.[15]

In the nineteenth century the minister of Kilbride, Alan McNaughton, recalled that,

> This stone was so carefully transmitted as a valuable heirloom, from one generation to another to another, that it was lost only within these few years, by being committed to the custody of a gentleman who partook too much of the scepticism of the age to have any faith in its virtues. It retained, however, some share of its credit, till its final disappearance. Some, even of the present generation, have had recourse to it for the cure of both man and beast.[16]

Another special stone was in the possession of farmer Robert Crawford of Glen Scorradale, Arran, in the second half of the nineteenth century, but it too is now lost. Many Highland families had some pebble or crystal and sprinkled diseased cattle with the water in which it had been immersed. Mackenzie mentions several stones with magical powers. Macphail describes three revolving globes of white marble which were kept on Iona for touching and which were called 'the Day of Judgement stones', — people believing, apparently, 'that when they had worn the sockets and pedestals by the continued motion of passengers that then the world should be at an end'. This practice again points to a possible connection between the Baul Muluy and that hollow stone receptacle below the 'Judgement Stone' of Molaise on Holy Island. The proximity of a spring on Holy Island is significant too, because associated with some of the estimated 3,000 holy wells in Ireland were certain egg-shaped stones, possibly pre-Christian symbols of fertility. On Kerry Head, in the remote south-west of Ireland and into modern times, the Corridan family have kept in a bag in their kitchen a stone said to remain always cool and moist even on the driest, warmest, days. When this 'Booley stone' was placed in the nearby well of St Erc, the power of the well was activated. An egg stone was also perched there atop a standing stone. Like the 'Clan-Chattons' or 'Mack Intosh' family of Arran, these Corridans were guardians from generation to generation of a special stone. In their recent study of Irish holy wells the Brennemans have discussed the phenomenological significance of such customs.[17]

The hermit's life

If Laisren's daily work and prayer were centred in a little cave warmed by the evening sun, his faith was quite compatible with the enjoyment of natural beauty. Woods rose around him on the slopes of Mullach Mór, where whitebeam, rowan and birch have long echoed to the cries of gulls, and his spring bubbled and ran to the sea. A hermit's existence such as this was famously celebrated, or even idealised, in early Leinster literature:

I wish, O Son of the living God, O ancient, eternal King,
For a hidden little hut in the wilderness, that it may be my dwelling.

An all-grey lithe little lark to be by its side,
A clear pool to wash away sins by the grace of the Holy Spirit.

Quite near, a beautiful wood around it on every side,
To nurse many-voiced birds, hiding it with its shelter.

A southern aspect for warmth, a little brook across its floor, A choice land with many gracious gifts such as be good for every plant.

A few men of sense — we will tell their number —
Humble and obedient to pray to the King:-

Six pairs besides myself,
Praying for ever the King who makes the sun shine.[18]

These verses are a reminder that hermits might belong to a wider community. So, were other caves on Molaise's isle inhabited and was there a central place of assembly? In 1549 Dean Munro wrote of a 'monastery of friars, which is decayed' on Holy Island. Old Ordnance Survey maps identify an area at the north end of the island as a 'monastery'. Traces of medieval structures have been discovered there. Although these do not date from Laisren's time, like many archaeological remains in Britain and Ireland they may mark the site of earlier wooden buildings which rotted away. Folklore has it that the soil about this area is different from that of the rest of the island and was actually brought from Ireland. Thus is echoed a similar belief that long ago certain women were employed to carry a quantity of holy earth from Rome to Blaan's establishment at Kingarth on Bute. At the 'monastery' site on Holy Island is a disused ancient graveyard, where burials took place not least because the island was considered safe from a wild hound which was thought to ravage fresh graves on Arran. The utilisation of monastic 'holy ground' for burials, even after the dissolution of the monasteries themselves, was certainly common practice in Ireland and lends weight to the Ordnance Survey's former categorisation of this site as a 'monastery'. The custom of burial on Holy Island is said to have been discontinued by the end of the eighteenth century, following an accident in which some mourners were drowned. With old Kilbride church in Church of Scotland hands after the Reformation, any subsequent use of a monastic site on Holy Island for burials was unorthodox.[19]

In 1840 the minister of Kilbride wrote that, on Holy Island,

> The situation of the burying place was pointed out by a number of rude tombstones which lay in heaps upon the ground; till two years ago, a modern utilitarian, who had none of Dr Johnson's reverence for sacred places, cleared the spot, and turned the bones and ashes of the dead to account, by rearing from them a crop of onions and carrots.[20]

About 1860 an old stone cross, just over six-feet high, was removed from the disused graveyard on Holy Island and buried in the grounds of the ruined parish church at Kilbride, behind Lamlash. Known by some as 'St. Bride's Stone', this was the same cross which was dug up at Kilbride in 1892 and erected in front of the new church in Lamlash village.[21] In 1908 Balfour saw grey slabs in the depression between the furrows of the ploughed burial ground on Holy Island and thought these to be, 'evidently the covering-stones of graves'. The present owners of Holy Island have planted some trees on part of the burial ground, which may yet yield significant archaeological finds. A research team from Glasgow University has recently recommended further investigation of the area.[22]

A shining light

That Laisren chose a hermitage which was exposed to view from both land and sea suggests that he set out to live by visible example rather than by quiet contemplation alone. On his island home, according to the extant medieval account of his life, Laisren 'shone with many signs of miracles' (S.7). He is still recalled on Arran in the name of the harbour and modern village of Lamlash. That the harbour and village are known by a name which is thought to be formed by the elision of the Scots Gaelic words for 'Isle of Molaise' ('Eilean Molaise') suggests strongly that Holy Island was once known as 'Eilean Molaise' and there is evidence which confirms that this was so. As late as 1912 the minister of the Free Church at Lamlash wrote that, 'the bay and district today are spoken of in Gaelic as "Loch-an-eilean" or "Loch of the Island"'. Shortly after the Great War an historian of Arran added that, 'people hereabouts who speak Gaelic still refer to Holy Island as "Eilean Molaise" and when they speak of going to Lamlash they say they go to Loch-an-Eilean'. A local historian, Colin Cowley, has suggested that Benlister may be, likewise, a corruption of Ben-lashrack. Benlister Glen runs up behind Lamlash.[23]

Headrick was unimpressed by Molaise's form of retreat. Following a visit to Holy Island at the beginning of the nineteenth century, he commented that,

> I could not help remarking that this saint, along with many others whom I have had occasion to specify, acquired his celebrity when dirt, nastiness and absurdity formed the most prominent features of sanctity. Had he chosen a similar cave on the opposite side of the island, where no boat could approach him, and where people from Arran could not get to him without danger of breaking their bones among the loose fragments of rock, with which the beach in encumbered, we might have believed him to have retired from the haunts of men in downright earnest. But he chose a residence where the channel is narrowest, and most easily accessible to Arran, and within the bay, where vessels from all quarters would find safety. Hence his object must have been, not to retire from the world, but to draw the world after him, and I doubt not but in this cave he displayed more pride, vanity and pomposity than Diogenes in his tub, or Bonaparte while seating himself upon a throne.[24]

The Rev. Charles Hall has remarked that 'this is expressive language, but strongly tinctured with the *odium theologicum*'. Among Headrick's other works is an 'Essay on manures' and his down to earth appraisal of Laisren is certainly pungent. Stripped of its judgemental quality it does raise a valid question about the nature of Laisren's stay on Arran. The saint might indeed have picked a more remote and bleak spot on the island, there being a number of caves on the north and east sides which seem capable of having served as hermitages. Perhaps he chose the cave which he did because he was expected in some way to minister to the people of Arran and to the sailors who dropped anchor in Lamlash Bay. There were many small oratories around the Scottish coast where chiefs and clansmen were wont to pray before and after voyaging. Either passively, by way of his exemplary lifestyle, or actively, by preaching and ministering, he may have deliberately made his home where it would be seen. Perhaps he tended a beacon. Keeping lighthouses and helping mariners were regarded as part of the duties of some hermits in medieval Scotland. Laisren's stay on the island was, according to the Salamanca manuscript, never intended to be permanent but was a step on his way to Rome. Those who encouraged him to follow that path, perhaps including Colum Cille and Fintan Munnu, may have wished to ensure that he became known to seafarers who dropped anchor in Lamlash Bay. Although it will be suggested below that Laisren treated himself quite harshly in later life, there is no reason to believe that the purpose of his retreat to Holy Island was to engage in extreme self-mortification or to dwell in complete isolation. As mentioned earlier, and although it may seem quite paradoxical, anchorites sometimes withdrew to a place of solitude even within the ambit of monastic communities. They were not necessarily required to live in very remote places, although some chose to do so. Certain great early Welsh monasteries were not built in the wilderness, as was later thought to be the case, but rather on once important highways which subsequently became less frequented or disused. Some islands were likewise more accessible than they may appear to us to have been. Travel by sea was then at times easier than travel by land.[25]

Whatever about keeping a beacon alight for sailors, it may be that Laisren occasionally lit a ceremonial fire on his boulder. The 'rock of the fire' ('creagan an tine') at Auchencairn on Arran was not only used for preaching. It was also a site where the 'need-fire' was made, cattle being driven through the flames for magical protection against disease. In 1912 a local minister wrote that hearths on Arran were 'till recent times' extinguished once a year and then rekindled from a sacred fire or 'teine eigin' which was produced at particular places by rubbing two pieces of wood together. This was in keeping with customs elsewhere.[26]

It is possible to imagine Laisren standing upright, arms outstretched as he recited the 150 Psalms as an edifying example of piety for the folk on Arran; or mounting his great rock to preach to the crews of the Dál Riadan ships as they assembled for action and to call on God for a righteous judgement to fall upon their enemies; or lighting a sacred fire; or tending a beacon for the home-coming sailors as they rounded the south of Arran; or warning of the approach of enemies; or towering above the accused or contesting parties, as they cowered in the precarious seats hollowed out of the Judgement Stone, their backs to him awaiting his decision; or spreading out his bread and herbs by his cave to enjoy a picnic on a nice summer's day. It is possible to imagine any or all of these things but, unfortunately, it is not possible to know if any of them actually corresponds to the reality of the daily life of the saint of Holy Island.

Headrick does not confine his unkind remarks to reflecting on Laisren and his choice of residence. He also asserts that 'traditions in Arran' had stated that Laisren retreated to his island because he was 'disgusted with the irregularities of his master'. However, there is no other evidence of such 'traditions' and, from what he goes on to write, it appears that Headrick mistakenly thinks that Molaise was one of those Laisrens who are mentioned in the old accounts of Colum Cille, whom Headrick also castigates. Those Laisrens appear to be quite distinct from Molaise of Arran.[27]

A strange story has also been told about a supposed disciple of Molaise, but this appears to be entirely fantastic. William Sharp, who wrote in the late nineteenth century under the pseudonym 'Fiona Macleod', penned many tales which were based on a concoction of folklore, history and imagination. It is not possible to ascertain if there is the slightest basis in legend or in fact for his long-winded account of 'Cathal of the woods'. This tells how the hot-blooded Cathal is sent by Colum to be with Molaise on 'the Isle of the Peak, that men already called the Holy Isle because of the preaching and the miracles of Molios'. Cathal falls in love with the daughter of a chieftain on Arran. Having been discovered in one another's arms, Cathal is then buried alive in a hollow oak tree at the behest of Molaise. He becomes a wood spirit. This tale of tension between pre-Christian and Christian traditions ends by the saint realising that he has been harsh and by him blessing Cathal and his 'fairy' family. The entire story is quite possibly a modern fabrication, with no basis whatsoever in fact or folklore.[28]

Less fantastic but perhaps equally misleading is an attempt by Knight to suggest that Molaise was a missionary in Scotland. This hypothesis is based on the assumption that a number of places take their name from his presence there, including Ardmaleish, near Port-Bannatyne in Bute, Kilmaglas or Kilmalosh up Loch Fine and Kirkleish in the Mull of Galloway.[29]

Admittedly a fiction is 'The tale of St Molaise and Neil' which was penned by Boyd Scott who, in his book on the east of Arran, alternates chapters of purported fact with chapters of imaginative prose intended to interest readers in the locality. As such his story may give us some idea of how Holy Island once was, if we believe that the saint lived with a community of monks there. The author relates how Molaise and young Neil, who is said by his creator to have later become the saint's successor as 'abbot' of Holy Island, defeated the evil lord of Monamore (Monadh Mór) on Arran![30]

In reality Laisren stayed long enough on Holy Island to be celebrated subsequently in the area and to be remembered in the calendar of Scottish saints. He had come, as the account of his life has it, 'with the intention of eventually travelling and reaching the apostolic threshold to see the relics of the saints' (S.7). The Arthur and Fitzsimon versions of his 'Life' state in particular that he wished to improve his knowledge by visiting Rome. It was relatively common during this period for Christians from Ireland and elsewhere to undertake a journey to 'the holy city', to see the tombs of the apostles and other sights. Some ancient verses gave pause for thought to anyone setting out on such a pilgrimage:

Téicht doróim
mór saido, becc torbai.
Inrí chondaigi hifoss
manimbera latt nífogbái.

To go to Rome,
Much labour, little profit:
The King whom thou seekest here,
Unless thou bring Him with thee, thou findest him not.[31]

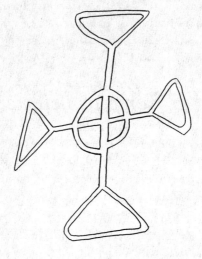

From a cross incised in rock above Molaise's cave

Holy Island.

View then the Bay by the majestic cone
Of Holy Isle, secure and peaceful made...
Shall we not Him adore, whose potent hand
Placed this stupendous bulwark in the deep,
'Gainst which the waves might spend their rage,
While safe behind the Isle in peaceful lake,
The weather-beaten ships, cheating the storm,
Might find a hiding-place and refuge sure.

-David Landsborough, snr (1779-1854).

CHAPTER 4

Via Rome to Leinster

THE ROMAN Empire had once stretched as far north as the Firth of Clyde, although it is not known if the Romans ever visited Arran.[1] Now, from the Firth of Clyde, Laisren travelled to Rome. It was his first visit to that city.

> (S.7 continued). When he came there, with God guiding his steps, he was received with honour by Pope Saint Gregory, and from him learned the volumes of both testaments and church laws, was ordained deacon and priest, and even consecrated bishop. He did not, however, receive all these honours at one time. At the request of blessed Columba [Colum Cille] and other holy men he twice went to the Apostolic City.

The Salamanca account of Laisren's life does not say how long he spent at Rome. However, both Arthur and Fitzsimon give the length of his stay as 'fourteen' years. The seventeenth-century Jesuit editors of Fitzsimon's 'Life' of the saint guess that this is an error and that Laisren spent four years, rather than fourteen, in Rome. Indeed fourteen years was the length of Gregory's whole pontificate, between 590 and 604.

Whatever the duration of his stay, it seems that Laisren was favoured by the Pope and received some training at Rome. The Salamanca 'Life' asserts (S.7) that his going to Rome was somehow connected with Colum Cille, who died in 597. That was also the year in which Gregory sent Augustine on his mission to the English. The other manuscripts do not connect Laisren's journeys with Colum Cille and do not have him made a bishop by Pope Gregory. However, all of the versions are agreed that his first sojourn in Rome culminated in a mission to Ireland:

(S.8) Also blessed Gregory, who ordained him, sent him enriched with
the text of the gospels to preach Christ in Ireland. While he travelled
through Anglia and Britannia and such lands, men who feared God on
hearing his reputation joined themselves to him — a large crowd of
outstanding men from different lands.

John Lanigan, author of a substantial history of the Irish church published
in 1829, doubted if in fact Laisren went to Rome at all at this time.
However, all of the old versions of his life state that he made such a journey
between his period of retreat on an island off the coast of Britain and his
return to Ireland.[2]

The kingdom of South Leinster

It was in Leinster, at Old Leighlin, and not in his native Ulster that Laisren
created that large monastic community for which he would later be
remembered. There is a hint of a connection between him and the well of
'Toberlastra' at Donaghmoyne, Co. Monaghan, because at it a holy person
called 'Lasair' has been recalled annually on 18 April, the feast-day of Laisren
of Arran and Leighlin. However, contrary to one report, the 'Lasair' of
Monaghan appears to have been female and, so spelt, the name is usually that
of a woman.[3]

Laisren's ultimate choice of south Leinster as the location of his
settlement was ostensibly inspired by divine guidance:

(S.8 continued) When he reached Ireland an angel ordered him to
direct his steps to the land of Lageniae, to a place called Lethglen,
where the city of Lethglenn now stands.

'Leinster' in the days of Laisren was centred on the valleys of the rivers
Liffey, Barrow and Slaney. Coastal areas were not then populated in great
numbers by the native Irish. The latter tended to sail up the rivers and
disperse in the hinterland, rather than settle by the sea. Although Maignenn
and Munnu founded monasteries near the estuaries of the Liffey and the
Slaney — creating places for those who alighted from ships there to receive
hospitality[4] — the eastern seaboard of Leinster was relatively unimportant
until the Norse later founded the towns of Dublin, Wicklow, Arklow,
Wexford and Waterford.

The old province of Leinster was also more confined than is modern
Leinster. It did not include to any great extent the land of the present

counties of Louth, Meath and Westmeath and was separated from the north midlands by the vast bogs of Offaly and by a zone of forest north of the Liffey. On its borders towards Ossory and Munster were heavily wooded uplands rising to the west of the Barrow. These hills above Leighlin were referred to in general as the Slieve Margy, a name which has now come to be used more narrowly. Moreover, the old province of Leinster was not only smaller than the present one. It was also composed of two distinct parts:

> Leinster was divided along the 'gabair' or watershed between the Liffey and Slaney — a line reflected in the diocesan boundaries between Dublin, Glendalough and Kildare in the north (Laigin Tuathgabair) and Leighlin and Ferns in the south (Laigin Desgabair).[5]

The southern area (Laigin Desgabair) is dominated by Mount Leinster and was steeped in history and mythology long before Christianity came to Ireland. The ancient fort at Dinn Ríg, located somewhere along the Barrow valley south of Carlow town, was the seat of the kings of south Leinster. One of the five lucky things listed by a scribe in the Book of Lecan was 'to drink by the light of wax candles at Dinn Ríg on the banks of the Barrow'. For at least two centuries the site of Dinn Ríg has been popularly identified as Ballyknockan Mote, close by Old Leighlin. However, the impressive earthworks which are clearly visible at Ballyknockan today appear to be later Anglo-Norman fortifications, although they may be superimposed on a pre-existing dún or rath.[6]

Whatever about the precise location of Dinn Ríg, it is certain that from this central region of the Barrow valley the ruling houses of both north and south Leinster set off on their respective careers of expansion. Laisren would have had little difficulty in reaching the area. The Barrow was long navigable as far north as Monasterevan, upstream from Leighlin and Carlow. An ancient road going north and south also passed through the Barrow valley. This route would continue to be of great importance after the Anglo-Normans came, when Waterford prospered as the administrative capital of Munster. The same road served subsequently as the main thoroughfare for mail coaches from Dublin, through Leighlinbridge, to Kilkenny and Waterford.

Leinster and the Irish Sea

Leinster in the days of Laisren was populated mainly by the Laigin, a distinct group of Celtic invaders who had, in the first flush of success, swept across north Munster and the southern midlands as far as the River Shannon. Their legendary high ancestor, Labraid Loingsech Moen, was supposed to have been king of Ireland and Scotland. At least one historian, F. J. Byrne, considers them to be identical with or closely associated with the Fir Domnann who 'can hardly be disassociated from their British [Celtic] namesakes the Dumnonii of Devon and south-western Scotland'. We have seen that Laisren's mother is said to have had a British uncle, quite possibly from the latter area. The Laigin were not the first inhabitants of Leinster whose ancestors were believed to have come from overseas. Thus, the Fir Bolg were said to have been forced out of the western isles of Scotland by the Picts, at some indeterminate time, and to have moved on to Leinster and thence to Connacht, before being expelled from the Irish mainland to islands such as Arran. There were actually some Picts in Leinster itself when Laisren arrived and, remarkably, like the Picts of Scotland, these are thought to have consisted of seven tribes or segments known as Loígis. The Loígis were believed to have been introduced as mercenaries and were settled west of Leighlin and Slieve Margy to defend a section of the 'midland corridor' between Munster and north Leinster.[7]

Further evidence of movement across the Irish Sea is provided by monastic place-names which indicate the presence of Britons in Leinster as an important factor in establishing Christianity there from the fifth century. Kuno Meyer refers to 'incessant intercourse' between British and Irish monasteries during the sixth and seventh centuries and adds that 'British monks and hermits in Ireland' became familiar figures, as did those from Ireland in Britain. The patron saint of Ferns, Co. Wexford — 'Edan' or 'Moedoc' — is said to have studied in Wales with St David. We know that Munnu came from Iona to establish his monastery at Taghmon in Wexford and Adomnán also tells us of travellers from Leinster arriving at Iona. The journey between either Dál Riada or Britain and Leinster was not particularly difficult, especially for the Dál Riada who lived by the sea and who knew well the ancient sea lanes which had long been frequented by the Celts. In his study entitled *Saints, seaways and settlements*, E. G. Bowen has spoken of 'a Celtic thalassocracy [Greek 'θαλασσα' meaning 'sea'], extending in early Christian times from Dál Riada to Brittany and perhaps even to Spain'. Indeed 'Greek strangers' held a market at the chief Leinster fair, known as Oenach Carman, and it is said that 'Egyptian' monks were buried in Ireland.[8]

Uí Bairrche

Returning from his first journey to Rome, Laisren disembarked in Ireland and made his way to an area which was then under the control of the Uí Bairrche. It is said that, 'the tribal name Uí Bairrche may also have a linguistic relationship with that of the powerful northern British tribe of the Brigantes'. In Laisren's day the rule of the Uí Bairrche appears to have stretched from Gabair in north Carlow down to the pass of Gowran, which leads from Leinster into Ossory. Their territory included centrally the valley of the River Barrow as well as, ostensibly, such historic locations as Dinn Ríg, Mag n-Ailbe and the site of the fair of Carman, although the precise locations of the last three are uncertain. Smyth notes that the name of the later Norman barony of Idrone (Uí Dróna), in which lay Old Leighlin, was misleading: in fact 'much of Idrone country once belonged to Uí Bairrche as far south in Co. Carlow as Lorum and across the Kilkenny border'. The author of the old 'Life of Munnu' suggests that Cormac, the Uí Bairrche king, was actually king of all south Leinster in the late sixth century, about the time of Laisren's arrival there, and that even Fintan Munnu's Columban foundation of 'Tech-Munnu' (Taghmon, near the later town of Wexford) lay in the lands of his tributary people. One Uí Bairrche princess from south Leinster married a northern Uí Neill prince and this couple became the parents of Colum Cille, whose important foundation at Moone in Leinster was just north of the Uí Bairrche territory.[9]

Dál Riadan connections with Leinster

Whatever about a Leinster princess marrying a northerner, it was unusual for Leinster princes to wed women from far afield. There were some exceptions and in at least two cases the brides were Dál Riadan. Thus Rónán, a seventh-century Uí Máil king of Leinster married the daughter of Eochu of Dunseverick, the northern stronghold of the Irish Dál Riada. For his part, Bran mac Conaill, the Uí Dúnlainge king of Leinster who died in 693, married Almaith of the overseas Dál Riada. The Dál Riada were of course Ulaid and the Ulaid and Laigin peoples were what F. J. Byrne has described as 'the hereditary enemies' of the southern Uí Neill at Tara. Cormac, the powerful Uí Bairrche king, had also a personal connection with Ulster. He left his kingdom in order to become a monk at Bangor.[10]

The monastery at Bangor had been founded by Comghall, himself the son of a distinguished Dál Riadan family who was deeply influenced by the

'Egyptian' monastic tradition and who died about 600. When Cormac gave up his throne and retreated to Bangor, he reputedly made to Comghall a gift of four places in the kingdom of the Uí Bairrche. At least two of these, 'Foibran' and 'Ardarema' have not been identified. Conjecture that one of these places might have been in the vicinity of Leighlin is enticing but ultimately frustrating. Comghall is said to have begun his own ecclesiastical and scholarly career under Fintan of Clonenagh, among the Pictish Loígis of Leinster and Flower believes that, 'whether this is true or not...it denotes a close connection between Bangor and Clonenagh'. Comghall's pupils at Bangor included Fintan Munnu, to whom Laisren as a child was possibly entrusted and who eventually made his way about 597 to Wexford by way of Iona. Columbanus, himself of Leinster origins, also studied at Bangor. There are stories which connect Comghall with Colum Cille and with Rathlin, an island sometimes closely associated with Arran.[11]

There is a persistent tradition which links Laisren's own grandfather, Aedán, with Leinster. He has even been identified as the son of Eochaid mac Muredaig, a king of Leinster, and Feidelm ingean Feidlimthe. One old story tells how twin boys were born to Eochaid and Feidelm, while they were once in exile in Dál Riada. At the same time another woman, who would come to be regarded as Aedán's mother, bore twin girls. She persuaded Feidelm to exchange a boy for a girl. Years later, it is said,

> Aedán [d.606] invaded Leinster but was induced to desist from doing battle with Brandub [d.605], when Feidelm had proved to Aedán that she was his mother and Brandub his twin brother.[12]

A poetic version of this tale praises Feidelm as being 'good at cherishing clergy and crosses' and has her protesting to Aedán that, 'by the most potent flagstone ['leicc'] in Scotland I am your mother!'. She promises him that his fame 'will be a full ornament for the Laigin'.[13]

The modern historian of Dál Riada, John Bannerman, thinks that, 'it is significant that Brandub mac Echach was of the Uí Felmeda, a people who inhabited the present counties of Carlow and Wexford'. Nevertheless, he adds, 'there seems to be no basis of fact behind these traditions'. Bannerman speculates that the traditions may owe their origin to an early relationship between Iona and the Leinster monastery of Tech-Munnu (Taghmon), founded by Fintan Munnu in accordance with a prophecy of Colum Cille and, as we have seen, apparently under Uí Bairrche control.[14]

Yew of Ross (Eó Rossa)

Leinster was steeped in its ancient pre-Christian culture, the memory of which long survived as popular folklore. In at least one important respect that culture was connected with the very place where Laisren was about to settle. For Old Leighlin is said by Eugene Curry and others to have been the location of one of the five great legendary trees of Ireland, the famous Eó Rossa, or Yew of Ross. Indeed, into the twentieth century, there long stood another celebrated tree at the cross-roads of Old Leighlin, by the village pub, and the place where it rose is still marked by a circular wall, within which now is a small stumpy tree. Whether or not this or any other physical location was precisely where the Eó Rossa grew is unclear.[15]

An old account of the battle of Magh Leana states that, on the night of the birth of Conn Of The 100 Battles, 'great fruit trees sprang from the earth in Érinn' and one of them was the Eó Rossa. A curious and beautiful rhapsodic litany of epithets, which is found in the Rennes manuscript of the Dinnshenchas, pays homage to this great tree. This has been translated by Whitley Stokes:

> The tree of Ross is a yew. North-east as far as Druim Bairr it fell; as Druim Suithe ('Ridge of Science') sang:
>
> Tree of Ross, a king's wheel, a prince's right, a wave's noise, best of creatures, a straight firm tree, a firm-strong god, door (?) of heaven, strength of a building, the good of a crew, a word-pure man, full-great bounty, the Trinity's mighty one, a measure's house (?), a mother's good, Mary's Son, a fruitful sea, beauty's honour, a mind's lord, diadem of angels, shout of the world, Banba's renown, might of victory, judgement of origin, judicial doom, faggot (?) of sages, noblest of trees, glory of Leinster, dearest of bushes, a bear's (?) defence, vigour of life, spell of knowledge, Tree of Ross!

Stokes says that he knows nothing of the singer, Druim Suithe, to whom this paean is credited. He describes the piece as a string of kennings, 'which in Irish, as in Scandinavian poetry, took the place of similes'. However, the force of the language seems to be stronger than that afforded by mere similes. Stokes adds of this litany that, 'it once perhaps had some meaning, now not easily discoverable'. It is not clear why Stokes was so puzzled. The litany is clearly a celebration of the Eó Rossa, Christian imagery being mixed with or overlaid upon that of the pre-Christian era.[16]

Another sign of this tree's special place in early Irish society was that it featured as half of the answer to a riddle with which Marbhán confounded Dael Duileadh, a member of the great bardic school: 'Which are the two trees whose green tops do not fade till they become withered?' When even a lesser sacred tree, or 'bile', might be regarded as an appropriate adjunct to a chiefly or kingly residence, then how auspicious it must have been if Laisren chose the vicinity of the legendary Eó Rossa for his foundation.[17]

A cult of sacred trees was widespread amongst the Celts and the Eó Rossa was one of the greatest of these. Evidently each tribe, or confederation of tribes, had its own sacred tree which stood on the site where the kings of the tribe were duly inaugurated:

> No doubt, like the universal World Tree, or *axis mundi*, the tribal tree was supposed in theory to stand at the centre of the tribal territory and to embody its security and integrity. Not infrequently one reads in the Irish Annals of a raiding force invading hostile territory and felling a sacred tree, and quite evidently this was conceived as a dramatic gesture designed to shame and demoralise the people for whom it was both talisman and 'crann bethadh', 'tree of life'.[18]

Just such a symbolical felling connects the Eó Rossa with Laisren, as we shall see below.

CHAPTER 5

Settled in the half-glen

I NTIMATIONS OF a connection between Dál Riada and Leinster, or between Britain and Leinster, do not oblige us to doubt that Laisren's footsteps were simply guided by an angel, as the Salamanca manuscript has it (S.8). Whatever the circumstances, he arrived eventually in the valley of the River Barrow. The Book of Leinster celebrates the saint's association with Leighlin ('Lethglend'). But, in verses which are at least eight hundred years old and pre-date the Salamanca 'Life', this text also refers to his abbotship of 'Rathcille', concerning which later writers are silent:

Mo Lasse lassar di thened
cona chlassaib tomaid
abb Ráthchille rí int senaid
m[ac] Maithgemme Monaid.

Molaisse, a flame of fire,
with the quires [choirs] in partnership,
abbot of Rathchell, king of the synod,
son of Maithgemm of Monad.[1]

Thus is the 'son of Maithgemm' (Irish: 'good Gemma') described as abbot of 'Ráthchille' or 'Rathchell'. There is no other known reference to Laisren being at a place called Rathchell and the location of this Rathchell is not specified.

In the very north of Carlow, about one mile from Rathvilly, is a Rahill, at which there are some remains of a church and graveyard and which is possibly so called from 'rath' and 'cell'. Perhaps 'Rathchille' was Rathkeale in Limerick or any one of a number of other locations with a name which derives from the common words 'cell' or 'coill', meaning 'church' or 'wood' respectively, and 'ráth', which indicates the defensive mound around an early house or fort. It may be noted that in Co. Wicklow on the Kildare border there is a small parish, sometime known as 'Rathtooll', which was earlier known as 'Rathozell' and which is said to have been in the gift of the medieval bishops of Leighlin.[2]

Barrow Valley Christians

Laisren was by no means the first Christian in the Barrow Valley. Indeed, St Patrick himself is associated with Leighlin, as he is with many other places in Ireland and Scotland. He is reputed to have paid an early visit and to have brought Christianity to the area, founding the monastery of Galen. There is a St Patrick's Well near Leighlin, at Ballyknockan, where St Patrick reportedly baptised converts. It is stated in the 'Life' of Laisren (S.9) that Patrick prophesied the coming of Laisren to Leighlin and his creation of a large community there. There is a tradition that St Fortchearn, 'who was smith to St Patrick', himself founded a monastery called Kilfortchearn in Idrone. In the fifth-century too Iserninus appears to have been based at Toicuile in Clíu, about nine miles north-east of Leighlin. Another indication of Christian activity is an old reference to a battle which is reported to have been fought in 488 at 'Cell Osnadh' (Kellistown), which is right beside Clíu, — the word 'cell' signifying the presence of a monk. At Agha, about four miles from Old Leighlin and about the same distance east of the Barrow as Old Leighlin lies west of it, there are very ancient church ruins associated with one Brandubh and possibly with St Fintan of Clonenagh. West of Leighlin, in the region between Slieve Margy and the Shannon encompassed by the modern counties of Laois and Offaly, certain important monasteries had been founded before Laisren reached Leinster. At Leighlin itself one 'blessed Gobanus', as we shall see, was head of a religious establishment when Laisren arrived there.[3]

A stop at Lorum

According to a local tradition, recorded first in 1869, Laisren did not make directly for Leighlin. He is said to have stopped first on Lorum Hill. This is about three miles south-east of Muine Beag (Bagenalstown), itself approximately five miles east of Leighlin. Lorum lies in the general direction whence Laisren would have come had he travelled overland to Leighlin from Munnu's foundation at Taghmon. Laisren, it is said, decided to settle at Lorum and only changed his mind when his path was crossed by a red-haired woman. Indicating in folklore an ill omen, this apparition was fortunately succeeded by an angel's voice which told him to 'go where you shall see the sun first shining and there shall your religious house be established'.[4] According to another version of this tradition, recorded by the Folklore Commission in 1938, Laisren went to the top of Ballycormac Hill at Lorum, one morning before sunrise,

> and there sat on a stone chair waiting to see on what spot in Co. Carlow the sun would first shine. The stone chair on which the saint sat was preserved there until about thirty years ago, quite close to the house now occupied by Mr R-. The present Mr R-'s father broke the chair and put the pieces in a fence near the house. Mr R-, according to his son's statement, was not aware that the chair was St Lazerian's. The sun first shone on Old Leighlin Hill.[5]

Stone 'chairs' were commonly associated with 'druids' and with saints, just as Laisren's 'Judgement Stone' on Holy Island was also known by some people as his 'chair'. At Lorum he was later recalled in the name of at least one holy well and there is even a suggestion that he was buried there.[6]

Continuing north-westwards from Lorum towards Leighlin, Laisren may have paused at Cluain na Ghalláin (Clonegall), or 'the meadow of the standing stone'. This is on the east side of the Barrow, immediately above the present Leighlinbridge, and adjacent to the site of an old enclosure, which was possibly a ringfort but which is now destroyed. The significance of this stone remains a mystery and it is tempting to speculate that there was a corresponding one on the west bank of the Barrow where the ruins of the Protestant church of Leighlinbridge now stand.[7]

At the end of the eighteenth century there were found at Leighlinbridge itself numerous burial urns which had been placed in low, narrow and long

vaults. These urns were made of coarse earthenware, capable of containing two quarts, and each was closed by a cover. They were under the garden or cemetery of the old Carmelite convent, which had been founded about the end of the reign of Henry III (1207-72). Inside the urns was nothing but dust. At the time of the find it was suggested that the urns had contained the hearts of devotees of the monastery, but they are more likely to have marked a much older burial site.[8]

Oenach Carman: a famous fair

It has been strongly suggested by Máire MacNeill, the authoress of a definitive study of the festival of Lughnasa, that Oenach Carman was held in the vicinity of Leighlin. Carman was the great triennial celebration for all of Leinster. Its equivalent in other provinces included the famous Oenach Tailten in Meath, Oenach Cruachan in Connacht and Oenach Emhain Mhacha in the territory of the Ulaid. The fair of Carman celebrated the festival of Lughnasa (1 August) and was an opportunity for the people of Leinster to attend to a variety of serious inter-sept business and religious ceremonies. There was a sacred funerary aspect to proceedings. The festivities included competitions in athletics, poetry and the other arts. To preside over the 'Games of Carman' was another of 'the five lucky things' of the Book of Lecan. Merchants attended from far and wide, a feature of the fair being 'the great market of the Greek strangers where there is gold and fine raiment'. It is not established beyond doubt where exactly the fair took place. In the 'double-kingdom' of Leinster it may have alternated between the north and the south of the province. In his study of Celtic Leinster, Alfred Smyth suggests that it was held where the Burren meets the Barrow, about five miles north of Leighlin. However, MacNeill examined the evidence in detail and argued that it must have been close to Leighlin. She based her case in particular on references to the event which are found in an ancient poem in the Dinnshenchas. This refers to 'the hospitality of Idrone' and implies that Carman was the focus for competition between the men of Leix, Forth and Ossory. Leighlin stands at a cross-roads between those three territories. MacNeill writes that Oenach Carman is possibly the same as Oenach n-Ailbe. The possibility that Mag n-Ailbe was located at or around the present Pairc Bán, east of Old Leighlin, is considered below.[9]

The Dinnshenchas adds that 'a burial ground for kings is its [Carman's] noble cemetery' and one is reminded of the major burial finds in the garden of the Carmelites at Leighlinbridge, which lay in Idrone. The poetic author remarks that many raths surrounded the site of Oenach Carman. In 1930 one local person who was interviewed for the Folklore Commission about Leighlin said, 'Raths are very numerous'. Might it be that Laisren's early foundation at Leighlin was itself once known as 'the church of the raths' or 'Rathchell', which we have seen to be an unidentified location with which the saint was long ago associated? The existence of ancient raths, or settlement mounds, is reflected in local place-names around Leighlin such as Rathornan, Ratheadon, Raheen and Raheenwood. From this latter townland west of the cathedral of Old Leighlin there is an old unused road, said to be inhabited by 'fairies' or spirits and leading to Old Leighlin churchyard. It is known as Bothar na nUaigh (Bothar na Nook, Bornanook) or 'Road of the Graves'.[10]

Saint 'Gobanus' of Leighlin

Crossing the Barrow, Laisren came to what is now Old Leighlin. South of the present cathedral a small stream runs down the glen to join the Barrow at Ballyknockan Mote, not far from Leighlinbridge. The stream is known locally as 'The Spa'. Within the memory of persons living in the late nineteenth century, the steep hills immediately south of The Spa had been shaded by a fine growth of old oak and by other primeval trees. In Laisren's day the whole district was heavily wooded and through its thick forests flowed the majestic Barrow, known from its nature as 'the silent river'. Up the hill west of Old Leighlin sits oval Raheen, now overgrown but formerly one of the largest ringforts in Co. Carlow.[11]

Laisren discovered an existing religious settlement at Leighlin:

(S.8 continued) The holy abbot Gobanus and his followers served God there. When he heard of the arrival of the man of God [Laisren], he went to meet him and after greeting him led him reverently to the monastery.

Immediately, we are told, the wonderful power of Laisren was made manifest to this 'Gobanus' and his community:

(S.8 continued) As they came to the door of the monastery, a certain woman then carrying in her arms the body of her son who had been beheaded by robbers, earnestly begged Saint Lasrianus in the name of God that he might restore her son to life. His feelings of pity were stirred by the lamentations of the mother and he turned to his usual help of prayer, and having placed the head beside its body he restored the dead man to life and gave him back safe to his mother.

Arthur and Fitzsimon (F.9) say that a cross was erected at the spot where the woman's son was revived and that this was called 'Crochcein' or 'Kroken', or 'Cross of the Head'. A gloss on Arthur gives 'croch-cín'. No such cross is recalled locally and the closest place-name today is Cruickeen, at nearby Mo(a)nmore. This has been thought to be from 'cnoicín' or 'little hill'.[12]

Clearly such wonders as the revival of the dead could not fail to impress people and it is said that Gobanus decided that he should yield Leighlin to Laisren:

> (S.8 continued) Then blessed Gobanus made a treaty of spiritual brotherhood with him, giving him the place and everything in it and setting up a monastery for himself in another place.

We know nothing of Gobanus or of his community. There were saints with this same name in the early church and stories of friendly personal contact are often included in medieval 'lives' as metaphors for amicable relationships between different monasteries. No such purpose seems to be served by this story, since Gobanus is neither well-known nor associated with any religious house which was later prominent or distinguished. We shall see below that certain sacred wood which was furnished by Laisren to St Moling was fashioned into an oratory only with the help of one 'Gobbán the Wright' who, in the details of the story, is indistinguishable from the famous 'Gobbán Saor' (also 'Goibhlann' and 'Goibhniu'), craftsman of Irish legend and mythical protector of Lugh. It was Lugh whose feast was celebrated at the Oenach Carman. Two other stories 'confuse' the 'Gobbán Saor' with early monks of the same name and, notably, these stories are all located in south Leinster. Daithi O hOgain, the folklorist, believes the monks' name 'to be a hypocoristic form of Goibhniu, the ancient god of smithcraft'. The Gobbán Saor became in legend a sort of friendly giant who helped to build castles and monasteries. Perhaps Giobhniu is represented here as 'blessed Gobanus' and the surrender by him to Laisren represents the yielding by an older learned class to the new. As we have seen, St Patrick's smith is also said to have founded a monastery in Idrone.[13]

Laisren opposed?

Both the Salamanca manuscript and the similar Fitzsimon account give us to understand that Laisren's arrival in Leighlin went smoothly. However, folklore recorded in the 1930s suggests that Laisren was not as welcome in the area as he might have wished. This relates that, on his coming, Laisren saw a glorious burst of sunshine light up the little glen and the oak woods surrounding it. He decided to build his church on Old Leighlin Hill:

> The owner of the land on top of the hill refused to give a site for the church or any part of the hill, but he offered the saint some very wet marshy land at the foot of the hill. The saint accepted this offer but

being very displeased at the owner's meanness he prayed that forever afterwards the land on the top of Old Leighlin Hill might be always wet and the land at the base of the hill (where he built his church) might be always dry. And so, people say, it is so until the present day.

Another story is that the owner's offer was that he could have an amount of land covered by his cloak and that the saint placed his cloak on the ground. It spread outwards till it covered the necessary amount of land suitable for a site.[14]

This version of Laisren's arrival raises the possibility that the name Leighlin, if it does indeed derive from the Irish words for 'half-glen', refers to the lower part of the glen which Laisren is here said to have been allowed, while the upper part remained outside of his control. It suggests that at least one powerful person in the locality was not easily reconciled to Christianity.[15]

Another version of the foundation story is that a local chieftain granted Laisren only a small lough above the enclosure of Gobanus. Laisren and his followers had to set about draining it in order to make room for their buildings. We are told that when Laisren spread his cloak over the lough its waters sank and almost disappeared in the clefts of the ravine. On the newly exposed northern bank there was ample space for Laisren and his monks to construct their dwellings and here today stands the cathedral.[16]

If Leighlin is indeed 'above' the enclosure of Gobanus, as this last version has it, then where was that enclosure? Was it on the fields to the east of Old Leighlin known as 'Pairc Bán'? Did the adjective 'bán' ('white') refer to some stone building or walls erected after Laisren's death but later mistakenly thought to be contemporary with him? Early structures of cut stone, such as the famous *Casa Candida* ('the white house') at Whithorn in Galloway, were perceived as 'white'. To people who had known mainly wooden buildings and palisades, dressed stone walls shining in the sun might appear brilliant or 'white'.[17]

Yet another local version of Laisren's arrival, recorded in 1937, left Gobanus out of the picture and thus avoided the need for any speculation about a predecessor:

The sun shone on Old Leighlin. When he reached the spot it was a pool of water. He blessed three stones and threw them into the pool and it dried up at once. Here he started and built his church. A well sprang up beside it to supply him with water. This is the well which is still in Old Leighlin.[18]

The name of Leighlin

Early manuscript sources refer to the place of Laisren's settlement as 'Lethglenn', or some similar Irish form which indicates that it derives from the words for 'half' ('leath' or 'leith') and 'glen'. This does appear to be the most likely explanation of the name. Today 'Leighlin' is pronounced by Carlow people as being somewhere between 'Lecklin' and 'Locklin', with a short first vowel and the emphasis on the first syllable.[19]

It is not clear when or why the area became known as 'Leighlin'. Fr John Aughney, the local parish priest, told the author that he could see it from certain angles as a 'half-glen'. The site is certainly tucked into a fold in the hills. I have suggested above that the 'half' may refer to the lower half of the glen, as folklore has it that Laisren was refused permission to build higher up a hill at Leighlin. Dineen states that 'leith' may mean not only literally 'a half' but, more loosely, 'a good share, a part or piece'.[20]

Beyond this point one engages in speculation. Thus, 'Lochlin[n]', 'Lochlann' or 'Lochlai[n]n' was a word commonly used by the Irish to refer to the overseas kingdom(s) of the far north in general, only later being applied to the 'Vikings' in particular. When spoken, the word can sound very similar to the actual pronunciation of Laisren's place of settlement in Carlow, namely Leighlin. Might it have been a local nickname for Laisren from Dál Riada, 'Old Lochlann'?

Then there is a Loch Léin mentioned in the Rennes version of the Dinnshenchas in connection with Luachair or Temair Luachra, the latter being identified as a place in Kerry. However, Luachair is known to have once included part of Limerick and a striking aspect of the relevant eulogy in the Dinnschenchas is that it refers in the one context to the Suir, Nore and Barrow rivers and to Loch Riach and Loch Léin. Loch Riach may be Loughrea in Galway but another lake of this name is in Leinster. The actual location of Loch Léin is unknown. There was too a mythical Loch Laiglinni, called after Laighlinne, the son of Parthalon.[21]

CHAPTER 6

Abbot Laisren of Leighlin

G OBANUS HAVING yielded to Laisren, the monastery at Leighlin continued to grow:

(S.9) Saint Lasrianus carried out the task given to him carefully, in everything distinguished, in everything well reputed. Outwardly a Christian people was thriving, inwardly a holy race was increasing; the small spring grew into a mighty river, because through the hard work of the holy man the number of believers multiplied to one thousand five hundred men. The strictness of their life and the strength of their virtues scattered the odour of good reputation through the whole island of Ireland.

Up to this point the Salamanca, Fitzsimon and Arthur manuscripts correspond quite closely. However, the last now becomes sparser in detail than the former, giving only an account of those incidents described below in paragraphs F.15 and F.18 and part of F.17. Fitzsimon agrees generally with the Salamanca manuscript as it continues:

(S.9 continued) What faithful Patrick promised in truthful prophesy came to pass about that place Lethglenn: 'After fifty [sic] years from now a stranger by name Lasrianus, a faithful servant of God, will dwell there'. And he added, 'The total number of holy followers will be as great as the number of their angels you see'. Patrick and those who were with him saw legions of angels filling that place. Also Saint Caynnecus [F.11: Cainechus] replied thus to certain virgins who were putting themselves under his care: 'It will come to pass that Saint Lasrianus will be your father and the father of many others'. In this way they prophesied about him.

The inclusion of such prophesies was a way for medieval biographers to bolster the reputations of their subjects. Patrick, of course, had lived not 50 but 150 years before Laisren arrived in Leighlin. In this reference to his prophesy, the number '50' may be a simple anachronism, a slip of the hand or a contemporary convention which signifies 'many'.

Visitors welcome and unwelcome

Persons who were later distinguished as saints in Ireland visited Abbot Laisren at Leighlin. They included Finbar of Cork:

(S.10) Many holy men gathered to meet him [Laisren] that they might have a chance of speaking to him and to be joined in loving agreement. The blessed bishop Barrus who was about to leave for Rome went to him then, and being honourably received stayed three days with him and gave him his right hand as a sign of unending friendship. The bishop Barrus said, 'I would like to leave some sign as a memento of our pact'. Lasrianus replied, 'Ask and God will grant it to you'. And holy Barrus said, 'You should ask for that because we have come to you'. Saint Lasrianus prayed and at once a bush produced nuts in abundance, from which the cross placed there is named. It was then spring time.

The Fitzsimon manuscript (F.12) specifies that it was a hazel tree which produced its fruit. The hazel represents wisdom in Irish tradition.[1] The cross mentioned here is not remembered in Leighlin today. Another saint who came to Laisren was Molua:

At one time the man of God, Molassi [Molaise], had a very bad sore under his breast and his mouth was twisted [in pain?] and he refused whatever treatment they were giving him because of the heavy heat and excessive bitterness. Hearing this, holy Molua came to him and said to him, 'If you permit me, I will bless your chest in which you are being tormented, dear father'. Then Saint Molassi said to him, 'Bless only with the holy sign and your prayer, but beware that you don't touch it in any way'; and so holy Molua blessing the chest of the man of God, straightaway the pain lessened from the root and the holy man appeared cured immediately. Then the two holy men with their followers gave thanks to Christ.[2]

Top: Dunseverick, Co. Antrim. Irish seat of the Dál Riada.
Crown copyright. Repr. with the permission of the Controller of H.M.S.O.

Bottom: Dunadd Hill Fort, Argyll. Scottish seat of the Dál Riada, from where
Laisren's grandfather ruled. Courtesy Historic Scotland.

Top: Cross on 'Judgement Stone', Holy Island, believed to have been incised by a medieval pilgrim. From Balfour, 'Ecclesiastical remains' (1908–9).

Bottom: Author at mouth of Molaise's cave, Holy Island, being interviewed for Radio Telefís Éireann. Courtesy Ani Rinchen Khandro.

Top: 'Monastery' site (centre) and burial ground (right), Holy Island, 1976. Also shows jetty, 'farmhouse', walled garden and 'wee house'. Courtesy Committee for Aerial Photography, University of Cambridge.

Bottom: Lamlash Bay and Holy Island from Lamlash, with Kay and Jim Morris who later sold Holy Island to its present owners. Courtesy Arran Banner.

Top: Old Leighlin, 'the 'half-glen', showing village, cathedral and site of holy well (circled), 1965. Courtesy Committee for Aerial Photography, University of Cambridge.

Bottom: Leighlin Cathedral, west end, from a sketch by Percy Vigors, 1843. Note gradual slope from west door to broken wall in the direction of the holy well, before levels were altered. Courtesy Irish Architectural Archive.

Top: Stone cross, hung with objects, at the holy well, Old Leighlin, 1996. Courtesy John O'Neill.

Middle: People at Mass at the Holy Well, Old Leighlin, 18 April 1996. Courtesy John O'Neill

Bottom: Medieval arms of the bishop of Leighlin (St 'Lazerianus' seated?). From Ware, Works, ed. Harris, 1739–45, at 'Bishops'.

Top Left: Stone cross at Lamlash, removed from Holy Island to the ruined church of Kilbride about 1860. Once at Cnoc na Croise? Shows Christ passing into a chalice from which His blood pours to a supplicant. From Balfour, 'Ecclesiastical remains' (1908–9).

Top Right: Detail of same, side-view, 1996.

Bottom: Medieval slab from Molaise's 'grave' at Clauchan, Arran. Mounted since 1889 in a wall at St Molios Church, Shiskine, Arran.

Top: Inter-faith service at Molaise's cave, celebrating in 1992 the purchase of Holy Island by Buddhists. Akong Rinpoche of Samye Ling speaking. Courtesy Arran Banner.

Bottom: Old lighthouse station and Mullach Mór mountain, Holy Island. From a postcard, 1911.

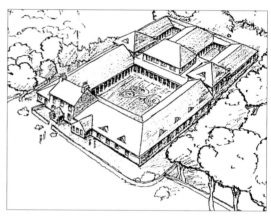

Top: Lama Yeshe, retreat master, prepares for a television interview at his new house on Holy Island.

Middle: Sketch of the planned Centre for Peace, Reconciliation and Retreat, Holy Island (incorporating old farmhouse). Courtesy Holy Island Project.

Bottom: Sacred Tibetan syllable, 'OM', painted on a rock, Holy Island, 1998.

St Molua or 'Lugaid' had a settlement at Clonfertmulloe, in what is now County Laois. This story suggests a connection between the two foundations at Leighlin and Clonfertmulloe and indicates that the densely wooded hills south-west of Leighlin, while serving as a partial barrier to the territory of Osraige (Ossory), did not prevent communications between the Barrow and the 'midland corridor', or 'Slige Dála', and the Shannon.

Not everyone who came to Leighlin treated Laisren with respect. To understand the significance of the fate that met three particular visitors it is necessary to recall what was said earlier about the fact that 'poets' in early Christian Ireland usually represented pre-Christian values and were in effect 'a protective metamorphosis' of the old Druidic order. Their satire was believed to have the power of raising blisters on the body of the person satirised.[3] Nevertheless, Laisren was not afraid of them:

> (S.11) Three poets came there with the intention of getting something and if not, then of defaming his character. When they shamelessly made their demand the man of God replied, 'I should not give you the property of the church but keep it for Christ's poor. To give it to tricksters is to offer it to demons'. As they left they began to mock him. But God, who punishes those who defame their neighbour, did not let this pass without notice. At once they were given the same sentence as Dathan and Abiron and were swallowed by the earth.

Happier, however, was the reception which a deposed monarch is said to have received at Leighlin:

> (S.12) At another time when the horse of King Edanus, who had been driven from his kingdom, was dying from lack of food, he [Laisren] saved it from the jaws of death.

Fitzsimon refers in this context to 'Aedanus' (F.13) and describes him as both Laisren's uncle (*avus*) and a king of Alba (*Albaniae Rex*). Can this be the same person referred to elsewhere in the same manuscript (F.1) as Laisren's grandfather and as '*Rex Scotiae*'? Based on a reading of the less embellished Salamanca manuscript, the historian John Bannerman has written that 'it is just possible', given the overwhelming defeat suffered by Dál Riadan forces at the hands of the Northumbrian king at Degastán about 603, that Aedán mac Gabráin abdicated or was deposed. Perhaps Laisren then sheltered his grandfather, saving his horse from the jaws of death. One source hints that Aedán mac Gabráin did indeed spend his last days in a monastery.[4]

The Easter controversy

Laisren is reputed to have turned his attention to a particular matter which greatly exercised the early Christian church. This was the mode of determining annually the precise date for celebrating Easter. There were various schools of thought as to the appropriate method of interpreting relevant lunar cycles and, as a result, Easter was observed on different dates in different places throughout Europe and the middle-east. The Easter question had been debated for centuries but, as the bishop of Rome came to dominate the organisation of the western church, orthodoxy was gradually insisted upon and local variations in church practice began to die out or to be suppressed. Church elders argued that the want of uniformity might occasion not only much inconvenience but also serious scandal. One continental group defied the new orthodoxy and clung tenaciously to the practice of celebrating Easter on the same date as the Jewish Passover, that being whatever day of the week the fourteenth of Nisan happened to be, and these became known as the *Quartodecimans* ('Fourteeners') and were excommunicated.

Adomnán writes that on a visit to Durrow in Leinster, Colum Cille prophesied that a great dispute about the matter would arise in time among the churches of Ireland.[5] This prophesy is a useful reminder that there were indeed 'churches' in Ireland and that Patrick's successors at Armagh did not yet enjoy the sort of over-arching authority which they would later come to exercise. Monastic communities in Munster and Leinster, in particular, may have traced their origins to missionaries who arrived in Ireland before Patrick. The successors of Colum Cille on Iona were also strongly independent. As a result, Irish Christians did not simultaneously adopt the Roman dating of Easter. Leighlin and other southern centres appear to have conformed early on, while Iona resisted to a much later date than did most communities.

In 628 or 629 a letter from the Pope which arrived in Ireland sought to have Irish Christians conform to the requirements of Rome in relation to Easter. In response to the letter Cummian, abbot of the Columban foundation of Durrow, consulted with the abbots of some of Ireland's most renowned monasteries and convened a synod at Mag Lene, near Durrow, to consider the matter. It was agreed to send a delegation to Rome and this duly departed. The delegates stayed in the same lodging house as a Greek, a Hebrew, a Scythian and an Egyptian, whose trustworthiness they regarded as being proven by the relics which they brought. The Irish were in St. Peter's for Easter, which that year fell a whole month apart from the date of its celebration in Ireland. Upon the return of this delegation, in 632, Cummian wrote to Segene, abbot of Iona. His letter is the only surviving contemporary document relating to this controversy in Ireland.[6]

To Rome again

It is conceivable that Laisren was a member of the delegation which Cummian mentions as having travelled from Ireland to Rome to discuss the Easter question between 630 and 632. Although the main manuscript accounts of Laisren's life do not refer to this controversy, they do record that he paid a second visit to Rome, at the bidding of churchmen:

> (S.13) When at the request of the holy abbot Kieran and other holy men of Ireland, in number fifty, he was sent to the Apostolic City for a meeting about church affairs, it happened that beyond the Alps he met a man who was troubled and very sad. But he who was accustomed to be weak with the weak delayed a long time (to find out) the cause of the tears and sadness, saying, 'You show such great sorrow, what evil have you suffered?' And he replied, 'I have family members who depend on my ploughshare for their support; today it was broken and I have no means or repairing it'. The kindly father said, 'A wooden...

At this point the Salamanca manuscript ends abruptly. Heist notes: 'rest missing, the following folio being cut away'.[7] It is from the Fitzsimon text that we find out what happened next:

> (F14, continuing S.13). The holy man told him to make a ploughshare out of wood and, blessing it, said: 'God willing, make do with that until my return'. He departed for Rome and remained there for a year and a half. The plough lasted that long and the head of the family harvested a crop as abundant as ever might a skilful farmer on fertile soil.

The language and style of the Fitzsimon account is somewhat more florid than that of the Salamanca manuscript and it differs from it in a number of relatively minor details, some of which were noted above. However, Fitzsimon appears to have been working from the same exemplar or source as was the author of the Arthur and Salamanca manuscripts, for both the content and order of these accounts where they exist are substantially the same. There is no reason to assume that the missing part of the Salamanca manuscript was not similar to the rest of Fitzsimon's version, and it is to the latter we turn to discover what happened at Rome.

Bishop Laisren

According to Fitzsimon, Laisren was only now made a bishop, ostensibly by Pope Honorius who was pontiff between 625 and 638. As we saw above, the Salamanca manuscript suggests that he had been consecrated much earlier, during the papacy of Gregory between 590 and 604. In the period when Laisren lived men appear to have been made bishops more readily than later and it was common for the same person to be both a bishop and an abbot. However, no records are known to survive which would allow us to ascertain when exactly Laisren was consecrated. By the time of this later visit, Laisren had already established a great monastery. It is quite possible that he was already a bishop. In any event, what is clear from all three versions is that he was believed to have been personally consecrated by some Pope and Fitzsimon's version adds that he was now further honoured by being elevated to the position of papal legate to Ireland:[8]

> (F.15) During his stay at Rome, the sovereign pontiff consecrated him a bishop and entrusted to him the responsibility of being papal legate in Ireland. But the more that he appeared laden with sublime honours, the more he humbled himself in all things and felt small. Truly, as the Saviour said, a town on a mountain cannot be hidden; because the more he conducted himself with humility, the more the Lord made him shine with the splendour of miracles. As he was returning to Ireland and found himself near Dublin, he remembered that he had forgotten the book of Gospels at the place where he had embarked, and he ordered holy Mochomet[9] to return to that place for it. That man obeyed immediately and Laisren said: 'Because you have accepted my order willingly, and so that your obedience may be an example for many, you will cross the sea on a stone'. The disciple then sat on a stone which he showed him; this serving the purpose of a ship, he crossed the sea and brought back the book which immediately Laisren gave to him as a gift.

This reference to 'Dublin' is an anachronism since there is no evidence that 'the black pool' ('dubh linn') from which Ireland's capital city takes its name was so-called in Laisren's day or that it was then the site of a settlement. 'Dublin' was later founded by Vikings and if there were prior settlements close to 'the black pool' they were probably at the ford of Ath Cliath and at Kilmainham. The Arthur and Fitzsimon accounts are in general more specific about places than is the earlier Salamanca version of Laisren's 'Life'. Thus, for example, they also state that Laisren's father was from 'Ulidia' or Ulster, whereas the Salamanca manuscript merely has it that he was 'of the northern part of Ireland' (S1, F1). Where the Salamanca manuscript omits to identify 'the native land' of Laisren's mother (S.2) or to identify where 'his own country was' (S.4), Fitzsimon gives 'Alba' (F2) and 'Ireland' (F4) respectively.

King of the synod

Cummian's letter of 632 did not mention Laisren and the manuscript accounts of Laisren's life do not include any reference to the Easter controversy. However, if he was a papal legate as reported (S.1, F.15), he could hardly have been excluded from such deliberations. Moreover, the Book of Leinster includes an old couplet which describes Laisren as 'king of the synod'. The text does not indicate what synod this was but the author of an ancient life of St Fintan Munnu writes that Laisren played an important role in promoting the new system of dating Easter at a synod which was held in '*Campus Albus*'. This synod appears to have been distinct from that convened by Cummian at Mag Lene. It shall be suggested below that '*Campus Albus*' is possibly the Latin rendering of a place-name in the vicinity of Old Leighlin.[10]

Fintan Munnu was perhaps that 'Mundus' or 'Munnus' into whose care Laisren is said to have been given as a youth, as we saw earlier, but this account of Munnu's life states that he and Laisren led opposite parties in the dispute over Easter. They are said to have treated each other with great courtesy. In this respect they were behaving in the exemplary fashion of Polycarp and Anicetus who, according to a fourth century history of the early church which is attributed to Eusebius, had calmly discussed the same matter in Rome four centuries before Laisren. Eusebius may or may not have influenced the author of the 'Life' of Fintan Munnu but his history is a reminder that the Easter controversy had exercised the wider church for hundreds of years. The Celtic churches were among the last to conform to Roman usage but there is no evidence that this conservatism reflected any doctrinal or ecclesiastical divisions peculiar to Celtic realms. Recent research in the limited documentary evidence available has demonstrated that standard church procedures were followed in Ireland for resolving the Easter difficulty when it arose. There may well have been Irish people who resented having to conform to practices which were being determined from beyond their immediate sphere of influence but it would be misleading to think of the controversy in terms of later concepts of nationalism or of Reformation politics.[11]

In reading the report of Laisren's involvement in the Easter question, which follows below, it should be remembered that Munnu is reputed to have suffered from leprosy for at least seven years, if not longer:

At one time there was a great council of the people of Ireland in *Campus Albus*, amongst whom there was contention [for a whole year] about the timing of Easter. For Lasreanus, abbot of the monastery of Leighlin, who was in charge of 1,500 monks, was defending the new order, which recently came from Rome; others indeed were defending the old. However, holy Munnu did not arrive immediately at this council, and all were expecting him; for it was he himself who was [first and foremost in] defending the old order. Then Suibne, son of Donald, chief of the Uí Margi region, said: 'Why do you wait so long for that leper?' Abbot Lasreanus replied to him: 'O chief, do not speak that way about holy Munnu; for, although he is absent in body, he is present in spirit. It is certain that whatever you say here, he hears it wherever he is now; and God will exact retribution from you for the injury to His family/servant (*famuli*)'.

On that same day, before evening, holy Munnu came to the council, and the holy men convened to honour him. When holy Lasreanus and holy Munnu greeted one another warmly, the aforementioned chief Suibhne advanced and sought a blessing from holy Munnu. The man of God replied to him: 'Why are you asking a blessing from a leper? In truth I say to you, that when you spoke ill of me, Christ, at the right hand of His father, was hurt/insulted (*erubuit*); for I am one of the true limbs of Christ and he himself is my head; and whatever hurts a limb makes the head suffer. From which, before the month is out, your own family will kill you and cut off your head; and your head will be thrown into the river Barrow and never seen again. And thus it was fulfilled. For in that same month the son of his brother killed him near the Blathae, a stream, just as the man of God had indicated (*vaticinium*).

Afterwards, holy Munnu said to abbot Lasreanus and all of the people there: 'Now it is time that this council comes to an end, so that everyone may return home'. As they were still in disagreement about the order of observing Easter, holy Munnu said: 'Let us argue the point briefly but in the name of God let us reach a decision. Three options are given to you, Lasreanus; the first is that two books be thrown in the fire, one of the old order and one of the new, so that we may see which of them escapes being burnt; or two monks, one mine, the other yours, will be closed up in one house and the house will be set alight and we will see which of them gets out of there intact; or let us go to the tomb of a dead monk who was just and let us revive him and he will indicate for us which Pascal order we must celebrate this year'. To him holy Lasreanus replied: 'We will not proceed to your trial; for we know (*quoniam scimus?*) that, because of the greatness of your work and holiness, if you say that Mount Marge is to move to the location of *Campus Albus* and Campus Albus to where Mount Marge is then God would immediately do this for you'. They were at that time in *Campus Albus*, near which is Mount Marge. Afterwards, the people agreeing with the holy men, they went home.[12]

An old Liturgy of the feast of Laisren, possibly late medieval, is not shy about Laisren's reputed role in the Easter controversy: 'As legate he decreed on what day Easter should be held and got rid of disputes. He brought back to the fold all the faithful whom schism had infected/deceived'.[13]

Whitefield, Pairc Bán and Mag [n-]Ailbe

The Latin name '*Campus Albus*' means, literally, 'White Field'. In his guide to early Irish historical manuscripts J. F. Kenney states that this synod of '*Campus Albus*' was at Mag [n-] Ailbe. Sources cited by Edmund Hogan, the authority on Irish place-names, indicate that '*Campus Albus*' may be a late and botched attempt at translating into Latin 'Mag [n-]Ailbe'. 'Magh' means in Irish a 'plain, campus or field' and the correct Latin translation would indeed be '*campus*', but 'Ailbe' is misleadingly rendered as '*albus*' ('white'). In fact 'Ailbe' seems to have been a proper name and not an adjective. Hogan's sources locate Mag [n-] Ailbe in what is now Co. Carlow, in the general region around Leighlin.[14]

There is close by Old Leighlin itself a large flat area which has long been called 'Páirc Bán' (or 'Baun'), which most obviously means 'white field'. This is a short distance east of the cathedral, across a road and beyond a farm, along the banks of the stream which is known at Old Leighlin as the Spa and at Ballyknockan Mote as the Ma[u]dlin. This Pairc Bán, in Moanduff townland, is taken locally to have been the site of the synod of '*Campus Albus*'. It is reputed to have been a location where, out of doors, clergy in white robes met to deliberate on many matters. In this context it may be recalled that Gaelic brehons also conducted much legal business in the open air. If this field was indeed the site of a synod, might it also have been the 'level sward for courses' of the famous fair of Carman?[15]

It would thus appear that the Irish 'Mag [n-]Ailbe' may have been firstly mistranslated into Latin as '*Campus Albus*' and then translated back into Irish, literally, as 'Pairc Bán'. However, a local historian, Martin Nevin, has suggested to the author a more obvious and simple explanation for the name 'Pairc Bán'. He says that the proliferation of white thorns in the area below Old Leighlin can be particularly striking when they are in bloom.

An entry in the Registry of Deeds for 1720 indicates that 'Park Bawne, lying and being in the town of Old Leighlin', may once have been an even more extensive area than the present 'Pairc Bán'. Perhaps all of the flat land along the river was formerly known by that designation.[16]

The term 'bán' ('white'), as has been noted, may refer to the bright appearance of dressed stone. The spellings 'Bawne' and 'Baun' which are found in the deed of 1720 raise the possibility that there was actually a Norman 'bawn' or castle standing here. It was suggested above that the remains of any such medieval structure could, after an intervening period, have reinforced or even given rise to a popular idea that the site of the earlier monastic settlement reputedly founded by Gobanus was below the cathedral of Old Leighlin where later ruins were to be found.[17]

In September 1996 the author met with the Connolly family who now own the Pairc Bán. Mr Eamonn Connolly, without prompting, told me that his father had told him that when he was a boy, about a century ago, slabs were discovered in the field when a horse was being buried there. They were left undisturbed and again covered. They may have been part of a religious or secular structure or a grave site. For their part the Connollys believe that a tunnel once connected the cathedral with Pairc Bán and Eamonn Connolly says that he once saw a lorry subside into some kind of a cavity in the field between the cathedral and the river. Below the north end of the chapter house there is a tunnel, crypt or very large drain going north and certain folk-tales have been recorded concerning subterranean passageways from the cathedral. Perhaps these simply led to the stream.[18]

When the area in and around Old Leighlin receives the sort of archaeological attention which it deserves then we shall learn more about the development during successive centuries of that great monastic site over which Laisren came to preside as abbot.

CHAPTER 7

The strange death of 'a noble deacon'

A S ABBOT and bishop, as 'legate of the Apostolic See' (S.1), Laisren expected deference from kings and chiefs. He is said to have dealt severely with those who displeased him:

(F16/ not in A) That remarkable man carried out his functions as legate in Ireland and confirmed by miraculous signs the authority which had been entrusted to him. By the power of his prayer, he healed the ulcerous foot of Felanus, king of Leinster, and he freed the latter from a demonic influence by driving away the demon. It happened that the king Cothinus charged a monk with robbing him; holy Laisren reproved him for that, and as the king delayed many days in making reparation for his act, the man of God prophesied to the Irish an immediate punishment for the king; the king died during the course of the following night. Again, Laisren finding himself in the territory of King Felanus, one of the servants of the king who had been sent to find water at the well refused to give a drink to the servant of God. On his return to the king's vicinity, the servant saw nothing inside the vase, and going back to the well he found no water there, and since that day it was impossible to find water there.

Laisren condemns his sister

According to a very old tale which is recounted in the book of Leinster, Laisren's wrath was such that he even damned his own sister when she had intercourse with a monk and became pregnant. The story has been dated to the early tenth century:

The sister of Mo Laisse of Leighlin was studying where Mo Laisse was. It was she, moreover, who attended upon the cleric. Now there was a young cleric in [Mo Laisse's] community. He and the young nun had sexual intercourse and she became pregnant. 'There will be bad consequences because of this', said the woman, 'if the cleric finds out. He will curse us so that we may possess neither heaven nor earth. But', she said, 'my ruination is enough. Go in order to avoid him'.

Laisren's sister promises not to speak of the monk, 'unless it comes through my side', and he in turn promises that, 'if I be alive, you shall not be in hell'. He then departs for Armagh. When someone later informs Laisren that his sister is in labour, Laisren retorts, 'May it be a labour of sudden death then'. Thereupon, 'he takes away heaven and earth from her':

That came to pass. She did not obtain communion. She went into the grave and hell. The cleric did not permit her burial in the churchyard. So, therefore, she was buried in the bog below the church.

Eventually, the monk with whom she had intercourse learns of what has transpired and, 'thereafter he proceeds to say her requiem, i.e. seven *Beati* [Psalm 119] every day; one hundred genuflections; the three fifties every day'. After that the young monk travels from the north. He meets Laisren and asks him for a small, secluded hut outside the church, in which he might beseech God. This request having been granted, he builds his hut near the grave and spends a year there:

One time, moreover, he saw her coming towards him.
'A blessing on your soul then', said she. 'You are good to me. I am almost saved'.
'What has saved you the most?' said the young cleric.
'The *Beati*' she answered.

The apparition then recites some verses which praise the efficacy of the *Beati* which 'is worth to the King who watches over us four and twenty cows':

On one occasion, moreover, the devout Fursa came to the church and he saw a ministration of angels in the bog going to the grave.
'Well, Mo Laisse,' said Fursa, 'who is the saint who is in the bog?'
'It is an idolater who is there,' said Mo Laisse, 'a demon nun'.
'Look at this, Mo Laisse!' said Fursa. He saw this, a ministration of angels rising from the grave towards heaven. Afterwards the body was taken from the bog and was buried in the graveyard. Fursa took the young cleric under his protection so that he made a saint and went to heaven.
Therefore it is that the *Beati* is better than all prayers.[1]

This story was obviously an encouragement to monks to recite all of the Psalms and in particular Psalm 119, which begins in Latin '*Beati immaculati*' and which has a certain mystical significance relating to the numeric value of its composition.[2]

Penned in a narrow hovel

It is impossible to ascertain to what extent, if any, this instructive tale about the sister of the abbot and bishop of Leighlin contains a grain of truth. There is found nowhere else a reference to the incident, or even to Laisren's sister. The story may have appealed to those reformers who lived two centuries after Laisren and who believed that the practice of Christianity had become less strict than in earlier times. Penance, denial and discipline were then being stressed as the means of keeping people on the straight and narrow path to Paradise.

If Laisren was hard on others, he was not easy on himself and it may be recalled that his own father was apparently 'stern' or 'harsh'. In one old account we find St Maignenn of Kilmainham, Co. Dublin, calling on 'Molasius' of Leighlin at the latter's 'house':

> Now Molasius was so that in his body were thirty diseases, and he (for devotion's sake) penned in a narrow hovel. Moreover he was thus: spread out in form of a cross, with his mouth to the ground and he weeping vehemently, the earth under him being wet with his tears of penitence. Maignenn said: 'I adjure thee by God, and tell me wherefore thou askedst of Him that in thy body there must be three score and ten diseases'. Molasius answered: 'I will declare it, holy bishop: my condition is revealed to me as being such that my sinfulness like a flame pervades my body [his name means in English 'my flame']; therefore, I am fain to have my purgatory here, and "on the yonder side" to find the life eternal. Knowest thou, Maignenn, how the grain of wheat uses to be before it is sown in the earth [sic]: that it must needs be threshed and beaten? Even in like wise it is that, or [before] I be laid into the grave, I would have my body to be threshed by these infirmities; and to God be thanks for it that, how near soever death be to me now, thou art come my way before I die. For God's love, lay me out becomingly; perform thou the order of my sepulture and burial'.[3]

Maignenn, as we shall see, is said to have later carried out Molaise's wish in respect of his burial.

Laisren and the yew tree

Meanwhile, it appears that Laisren turned his attention to a certain yew tree in Leinster, although whether or not this was the famous Eó Rossa is not specifically said:

> (F.17) There was in Leinster an immense yew which performed no useful service for the Church. Certain people, all of them holy men of Ireland, each wished to have it to construct a church, but there was such a degree of fraternal charity amongst them that no one ventured to cut down for themselves a tree which he knew was desired by another. So that such a tree would not appear to have grown in vain, they decided that each would take a turn to approach the tree with his disciples and offer to God fasting with prayers, and the tree would fall at the turn of that man whose life the Lord judged to be the most worthy. Each one fasting near the tree, the roots began to move and when Laisren fasted with his disciples, the tree fell. The others were asking if it was necessary to give all the wood to Laisren, for during their fasts, they had seen the movement of the roots prepare the fall of the tree. They entrusted themselves then to the judgement of the holy king and pontiff Cranmalus. Two stags having been captured on the hunt, Cranmalus decided that a plank would be attached to them and that wherever they went, all of the tree would be transported. This was done and God directing the affair, the stags transported the plank to the monastery of Leighlin, and all the rest of the tree was brought there.

If the story of Laisren and the yew tree was intended to be taken to refer to the Eó Rossa then it is perhaps best understood as a symbolical enactment of the religious conversion or ideological conquest of pre-Christian Leinster. It may be compared with a random tale in the Lebar Brecc, at entries for 20 April:

> A great tree was in the world in the east, and the heathen used to adore it, and the Christians fasted against all the saints of Europe that the tree might fall, and forthwith it fell.[4]

The Fitzsimon version is the only 'Life' of Laisren to include the story of the yew and it does not specifically identify it as the Eó Rossa. However, there is another and older manuscript which states that the Eó Rossa became the property of Laisren, albeit by falling in a gale and not by the power of prayer. This source is an old 'Life' of Saint Moling, the manuscript of which is in

Brussels. Moling had his settlement at Tech Moling (St. Mullins) on the borders of Carlow and Kilkenny, along the Barrow just south of Leighlin. According to the later editor of Moling's 'Life', the saint spent many years of his life travelling around with a wallet and bowl, 'like a Buddhist monk'. The story of his receiving wood from Laisren is particularly striking because of the involvement of 'Gobbán the Wright':

> At that time then, the yew of Ross fell, and Molaisse distributed it to the saints of Ireland. So Moling went to ask him for some of the Yew of Ross. Of the tree Molaisse gave him the roofing of his oratory. Then Moling brought Gobbán the Wright to build his oratory. Eight wrights [makers or builders] had Gobbán, and eight women, and eight boys. They remained to the end of the year, and nought they did for him, yet none the worse their entertainment.

Before the oratory was finished Moling fell out with the wife of the Gobbán and she told her husband that she would never lie with him again unless he got in satisfaction the fill of the oratory in rye-grain. This he got, and a description of his inversion of the completed oratory and its filling with grain is given. The building is referred to as 'the brown oratory', presumably because of its revered wooden roof. The modern editor of Moling's 'Life' discerns a trace of tree worship in this mention of the Eó Rossa. The story may also signify some form of exaction by the old order from those Christians who wished to build new places of worship.[5]

Yet another great tree may have fallen in or near Leighlin, if indeed Leighlin was in the vicinity of Mag Ailbe. This was the Mag Mugna. That references to these trees has an immediate mythological dimension is underlined by one description of the Mugna as being 'a vast tree, the top whereof was as broad as the whole plain' of Ailbe. It was said to stand 'on the brink of the Barrow' and to be thirty cubits in girth and 300 cubits in height, bearing fruit thrice a year, including 'apples, wonderful and marvellous; nuts, round, blood red, and [600 sacks of] acorns, brown, ridgy'. It fell southwards over Mag Ailbe from the vicinity of the modern village of Moone, site of a Columban monastery.[6]

The oratory and the shepherd

While Moling built one oratory. Laisren built another. This story is told by both Fitzsimon and Arthur, the latter specifying that Laisren's oratory was 'in the ecclesiastical town of Leighlin':

(F.17 continued) As Laisren was looking for an architect to construct an oratory, a shepherd said: 'If only I was a craftsman, I would make it free of charge'. And Laisren answered; 'God can easily instruct you, if He pleases in His goodness'. And having laid his hands on him, he blessed him and made him capable in the art of construction; the shepherd then built a very beautiful oratory, and as Laisren prepared to dedicate it, the citizens of the heavenly Jerusalem sang during the night of the dedication, and the sweet melody of that concert echoed in distant ears.

Death and a druid

If Laisren managed to avoid being hit by the various falling trees of south Leinster, he could not escape death itself. This came to him, according to various annalists, between 638 and 641. Both the Arthur and Fitzsimon manuscripts conclude almost identically, recalling the saint's passing:

(F.18) The blessed Laisren having demonstrated by these marvels, and by others which it is impossible to relate here, that he was the divine temple of the Holy Spirit, got ready to receive the reward for his merits: on the fourteenth of the kalends of May, he was summoned into the abode of eternal light where he was surrounded by the glory of eternal light, all venerating him with piety and imploring with confidence the clemency of the Saviour, Jesus Christ, Our Lord to whom, with the Father and the Holy Spirit, is honour and glory throughout the ages. Amen.

We must look beyond the accounts of Laisren's life for further details of his death. Elsewhere we find an ancient story of how Laisren died and it is quite extraordinary. As related by Oengus it involved an unhappy meeting between the abbot of Leighlin and Saint Sillán of Imbluich in Cualnge (possibly Emly, Co. Louth), whose feast-day the church used to celebrate on 11 September each year and who appears to have been a sort of vehicle of euthanasia. Thus, at the entry for Sillán in the 'Felire Oengusso' we read that Sillán was the '*salm*, i.e.*oratio*, of every feeble one',

i.e. every one who used to be in sore sickness: for this was the wish of them all, to see the hair of Sillán's eyebrow so that they might die swiftly, for this was the peculiarity of that hair, every one who would see it in the morning died at once. Now Sillán happened (to come) to

Lethglenn, and Molaisse comes early in the morning round the graveyard. Sillán of the Hair happens to meet him. 'This hair', says Molaisse, 'shall not be killing everyone', plucking it out perforce. Then Molaisse, after seeing the hair, dies at once, and hence Sillán, *dictus est* (Sillán of the Hair).[7]

It is difficult to know what to make of this ancient story. Sillán's eyebrow may be a variant of that 'evil eye' which is common in folklore. For example, W. M. Mackenzie has written of a persistent belief in 'the evil eye' on Arran and noted that, 'even good men could have the evil eye through no fault of their own. A minister at Kilmore always had to invoke the blessing of God on his cattle every time they came under his eye to save them from its evil effect'. There were also those 'who by unholy art could cure diseases beyond the power of the regular doctor. One fatal effect followed every cure: the first living thing on which the eye of the performer alighted fell down dead'.[8]

More speculative would be the placing of a construction on this tale which saw in the person of Sillán, for all of his attributed holiness, some kind of Druid or 'poet'. We saw that Colum Cille was famously celebrated by the old poets because he reputedly encouraged his contemporaries not to expel them. Did Laisren, who seemingly differed from Iona on the vexed question of the timing of Easter, also differ from his grandfather's spiritual adviser on the degree of toleration to be extended to the old order? Thus, he was associated with the destruction on the ancient sacred tree of Leinster and we have seen fierce retribution visited on three 'poets' who threatened him with malediction. Does this story of Sillán suggest that another such confrontation proved fatal for Laisren? The reference to Sillán's soubriquet, 'of the Hair', and another to Sillán's 'poisonous hair' may be significant in that it has been noted that, 'there are indications that they [the poets] affected a distinctive hair style'. It is perhaps for this reason that those who took Rome's side in the debate over Easter and certain other matters attributed the old Celtic tonsure (monastic 'haircut') to Simon Magus, arch-opponent of the early apostles and reputed collaborator with the Druids.[9]

The earliest surviving reference to Laisren is in fact a record of his death. It is found in the Martyrology of Oengus, which was written over 1,000 years ago, and is entered at '18 April'. This date, as we saw, is Laisren's feast-day in Ireland and Scotland:

On the feast of Septimus,
A noble deacon,
Laisren, victorious flame,
gentle abbot of Lethglenn,
(was declared to be) solaced (gone to heaven).[10]

　　Laisren is said to have asked Saint Maignenn of Kilmainham to take care
of the arrangements for his burial, as was noted above. From an old account
of the life of Maignenn it appears that Laisren's funeral was a remarkable and
important event:

> Accordingly Maignenn carried out the order of these obsequies, which
> made the third most exalted burial that was done in Ireland: Patrick in
> 'dún dá leth nglas' [Downpatrick]; Mochuda in Raithin of O Suanaig;
> and Molasius, that by holy bishop Maignenn was buried.[11]

Laisren having died between 638 and 641, some writers state simply that he
was buried under his church at Leighlin. We cannot be sure where that
church was and nothing indicates any such burial site. Nor is there further
evidence that his funeral service was indeed as striking as is suggested by the
extract from the 'Account of Maignenn' given above. Of course, the absence
at Leighlin of any monument or tomb of Laisren may simply be explained
by the fact that the earliest monastic structures subsequently fell into decay
or were destroyed. In any event, it is not common for the exact burial place
of saints of this period in Ireland to be identified. As already stated, some
people thought that the saint was actually interred at Lorum in Co. Carlow.

Laisren's grave on Arran

For their part, the inhabitants of Arran have long believed that Laisren, or
'Molios' as he is today better known to them, was buried on their island, at
Clauchan Glen, which lies over by Macrie Moor and Shiskine on the west coast.
This has been the outstanding farming area of Arran since prehistoric times, its
importance being underlined by the fact that at Shedog near Clauchan two fairs
used to be held annually. It is said that the saint returned to Arran late in life and
lived to the ripe old age of 120. He is believed to have founded a little chapel at
Clauchan and for many centuries a site in the centre of Clauchan cemetery was
venerated as his resting-place. His 'grave' there was long covered by a carved
medieval slab, ostensibly sculpted many years after his death. A holy well in the
vicinity of Shiskine, about a mile from Clauchan, was also associated with him.[12]

Obviously Laisren cannot have died in two places but it is possible that at least a part of his remains were brought back to Arran after his death, the bodies of medieval saints sometimes being divided. Any suggestion that 'St Molios', who for so long has been revered at Clauchan and Shiskin, was a different person from the saint of Holy Island runs contrary to the traditional belief of people who live on Arran, as given expression in the accounts which follow and as further considered in the appendix below where forms of the saint's name receive attention.

About 1772 that old slab or tombstone which had long lain on the saint's 'grave' of Clauchan was broken 'by some sacrilegious fellow in search of treasure; but an islander, who stood by, assured me that the attempt did not go unpunished, for soon after the audacious wretch was visited with a broken leg'. In 1807 Headrick wrote that, 'his [the saint's] grave is shewn in the burying ground, being a stone coffin, covered with a flat stone'.[13]

On the flat grave-stone on Arran there had been carved the image of a monk. In 1845 a local Protestant minister wrote that,

In the middle of the burying ground at Cla[u]chan, is the grave of St Molios. His first residence was in the island of Lamlash, or the Isle of Molios; but he afterwards removed to Shisken and fixed his residence where now repose his remains. He died here at the advanced age of 120... the stone which covers his grave is said to have been brought from Iona. Till within the last fifty years, it was customary for females after their confinement, to repair to the grave of the saint and there deposit upon the stone a silver-piece as a thank-offering for their recovery.[14]

In 1873 McArthur observed that,

The traditional Cla[u]chan of 'Saint Molios' is supposed to have occupied the site of the present chapel at Shisken [that 'present' Church of Scotland chapel in Clauchan Glen is today a ruin]. It is marked in Blaeu's map [of 1654] as Kilmichael. The old churchyard still remains with its primitive tombstones. Near its centre there is the Stone of St Molios, said to have been brought from Iona, sculptured with the figure of the Saint arrayed in the robes of a mitred abbot, with pastoral staff by his side and chalice in his hands. There is nothing improbable in the supposition that the body of Saint Molios may have been brought from Ireland to the island where he is said to have passed the early years of his manhood, and been buried there, in the little secluded cemetery of the Cla[u]chan. The Arran people fondly cling to the time-honoured traditions of their patron saint; and we would not rudely strip from the old burial-place the sacred association which has consecrated the dust of so many generations.[15]

Did the Cistercian monks of Saddell on Kintyre once cover the reputed grave of Laisren with its carved slab? Their foundation, said to have been established by the Irish Cistercians of Mellifont, lay a very short boat journey across a sound from the west coast of Arran. Two Cistercians, John and Herlewin, were bishops of Leighlin itself from 1198 to 1216, the present cathedral there having been begun around 1165. We do not know if they or their brethren at Mellifont fostered those pilgrimages to Arran and Holy Island which are believed to have been common in the Middle Ages. What is certain is that in the Middle Ages the house at Saddell was endowed of the lands at Shiskine and it is recorded that between 1164 and 1204 Ranald, lord of the isles, founded 'a religious order of Molaise', concerning which nothing else is known but which may have been connected with the ruined 'monastery' on Holy Island. It is thought probable that there used to be a regular ferry from Ireland to Kintyre and it may be that Irish travellers came to 'The Pilgrims' Way' on Arran via the Cistercian monastery on Kintyre. In any event, some medieval sculptor made that grave slab which still survives and which shows a man in simple ecclesiastical robes with chalice and staff.[16]

In the first volume of the *Book of Arran* Balfour argues persuasively that the style of decoration on the tomb on 'Molaise's gravestone' is that of a date much later than the death of the saint. He points out that the figure is clearly depicted as a medieval ecclesiastic and suggests that there can be little doubt but that what we see is an abbot of the Cistercian house of Saddell, about 1257. What he does not explain is why such an abbot would have been buried not at Saddell but at Shiskine and why he merited such a monument, one which Balfour accepts is much earlier than any comparable representation found on the Scottish isles. Were the Cistercians burying one of their own, or honouring a saint beloved by the people amongst whom they came? Balfour does not address the possibility that the tomb was made to mark an older and venerated site. In the Middle Ages the surviving Latin 'Life' of Laisren was written and he then enjoyed his own liturgy as one of the leading saints of Leinster. The buildings of which traces remain at the 'monastery' site on Holy Island may also date from this period.[17]

In 1873 McArthur included with his account a sketch of the grave-stone which shows it to be that which a few years later was moved and incorporated into the wall of the present Church of Scotland church in Shiskine, where it still remains. Balfour gives the date of this transfer as 9 July 1889. The modern building is a beautiful little structure which stands about a mile south-west of its antecedent and the fact that local Presbyterians took the cracked tombstone from their saint's grave and moved it such a distance, presumably to preserve it, underlines the abiding power of his presence. That members of a Church so adverse to statuary and the cult of saints, which does not even celebrate Laisren's feast-day, have erected his purported grave slab on the wall of their chapel and called that chapel by a form of his name is eloquent tribute to his fond place in the folk-memory of Arran.[18]

The Pilgrims' Way

The saint's 'grave' at Clauchan came to be greatly honoured by pilgrims from Arran and beyond who used to walk the island on foot from one holy site to another. They followed a path which is still known locally by older people as 'The Pilgrims' Way'. From the west coast this went up Clauchan Glen, over by the Hill of the Cross (Cnoc na Croise), down the Hollow of the Cross (Lag na Croise) and through Benlister Glen to ancient Kilbride church and Lamlash Bay in the east, whence boats left for Holy Island. The 'Way' was seven or eight arduous miles long.

According to tradition, Cnoc na Croise was the resting place of Molaise whenever he went from his cave on Holy Island to his chapel at Clauchan. 'The Pilgrims' Way' does not appear in recent guides to walks on Arran and the author of one published about 1976 indicated that, by then, its route could only be found with some difficulty, due to afforestation. He wrote that, 'there is little track left to see or follow'. However, in April 1998 the author struck out alone on foot up Clauchan Glen through the forestry plantation. Walking for about an hour on a good vehicle track, it was quite easy to reach the far side of the plantation by Clauchan Water. There appeared to be no impediment to continuing up this quiet and deserted glen. A local farmer, Mr Don Robertson, told me later that one simply follows Clauchan Water to its head and then, about half a mile later, one meets the head of Benlister Burn and descends. Long before the island's only present transverse roads opened, 'The String' and 'The Ross', this path connected the two most populated and important areas of Arran, namely Lamlash and Shiskine.[19]

It may be assumed from its name, 'Hill of the Cross', that on top of Cnoc na Croise there once stood a cross, perhaps even that which is today outside the modern church in Lamlash village. The fact that this old cross in Lamlash was found buried at Kilbride, and is said to have been unearthed even earlier from the disused cemetery on Holy Island, does not rule out the possibility that after the Reformation it was removed from Cnoc na Croise for safe-keeping. Many images were destroyed by religious reformers in Scotland. An historian of the church on Arran writes of medieval pilgrimages to the shrines of saints that,

> Crosses were erected at places where the travellers caught the first glimpse of these venerated resorts. Here pilgrims knelt and said the *Pater Noster* [Our Father]. In the case of Strathblane a cross was erected on the top of a hill which marked the spot where the church first comes into view to people who were approaching from the west.[20]

CHAPTER 8

Molaise's holy wells

T HERE ARE two particular holy 'wells' or springs which even yet are
associated with Laisren, or 'Molaise' as the saint is more commonly
known in this context. One well is on Holy Island and the other is
at Old Leighlin. Both were traditionally believed to have curative properties,
as was a third at Shiskine. Few visitors today expect to be healed miracu-
lously at the wells. Some allow that the waters might contain a beneficial
mineral or other natural agent or that the springs' association with Laisren
may have some psychosomatic or spiritual effect on believers. Others live in
hope and take a drink 'just in case'.

The well on Holy Island

The spring on Holy Island is slightly south-west of the saint's cave, just
beyond the enigmatic 'Judgement Stone'. It is close to the shoreline, its water
issuing across the path which runs along the edge of the island and draining
down through boulders and rocks to the bay. In 1768, in the course of his
tour through the western isles, Robertson visited Holy Island. He observed,

> one well in particular, called St Maolisa's [sic] well, with a bathing
> pond, which the natives used to drink and to bath in for all lingering
> ailments...It contains no mineral, but is entirely pure, gushing out of
> a rock.[1]

Not long afterwards Thomas Pennant made the same journey and referred
to Molaise's 'well of most salutary water, a place for bathing'. In 1807
Headrick, following in Pennant's footsteps, found that a cistern had been
constructed at the well:

> Adjoining to the cave, there is a spring of very pure water, for which
> a cistern has been built of masonry, with a stone spout which delivers

the water. This spring has been long celebrated for its miraculous cures of every disease incident to the human frame; and people come from very remote distances to bathe their debilitated limbs in the cistern, or to imbibe its life-restoring water from the spout. This miraculous power was supposed to have been conveyed to the water in consequence of the prayers and benedictions of the saint: and though the spring has long ceased to work miracles, the people still entertain for it a sort of superstitious veneration.[2]

There were, unsurprisingly, other springs on Arran which were also believed to be special. One of these was Bab's Well, on the road from Lamlash to Brodick. However, it was to Molaise that the Kelso family resorted early in the twentieth century. They were tenants on Holy Island and one of them later recalled that,

Father died on Holy Isle: there was a well on the island which was supposed to have healing properties, and my father expressed a wish for water from the well, so I went each day and got a fresh supply, but to no avail: he died.[3]

There is a belief on Arran that 'The Saint's Bath', which was possibly part of the arrangement which included a cistern and spout, was removed from Holy Island in 1918, the last year of the First World War, by relic-hunters from an American minelayer anchored in Lamlash Bay. In 1994 an archaeologist visiting Holy Island found the well in good condition, but 'the remains of the cistern are obscure by plant growth, as is the source of the spring. It is being well maintained'.[4] There is now no trace of the old spout. Some pinkish-white stones, which have been placed in the stream by Buddhist nuns, are particularly attractive when the sun shines. A scoop has been left at the side of the stream for visitors and the spring water is still highly regarded by some of those who have visited and stayed on the island in recent years.

If there was a body of folklore relating to the well on Holy Island, it does not appear to have survived. Balfour does not pay the spring much attention. The fact that the island was long a place of pilgrimage and a burial ground does not necessarily mean that those who came to Holy Island in the centuries after Molaise revered his holy well as a source of healing, but its reputation in this respect seems quite likely to be of great antiquity.

The well at Old Leighlin

Fortunately, thanks to the work of the Irish Folklore Commission, there is a record of the traditions which have been associated with the spring of Old Leighlin. As earlier indicated, there is a legend which has it that this particular spring burst out of the ground the moment Laisren arrived.[5]

The spring at Old Leighlin emerges about 200 yards west of St Laserian's Cathedral and, according to folklore, a secret tunnel links the cathedral and the well. The cathedral eventually became the property of the Church of Ireland, unlike the area around the well which continued to be frequented by those who were not Protestants. Drinking from it remained a way of being connected to the older order, perhaps not only that which had existed before the Reformation or that of Laisren's monks but even that which prevailed before the coming of Christianity. This connection may explain the story of the 'secret tunnel'.

People in Co. Carlow today speak of 'St Laserian' rather than 'St Molaise'. However, they do talk of 'going up to Molaise' when referring to a trip to the spring and the annual ceremonies every 18 April are known as 'The Molaise'. In the 1860s, according to the late Fr O'Hanlon, the 'peasantry' used to call the spring 'St Molshi's Well'. There are still people in the district whose first name is Laserian and for years the boys in the parish generally took Laserian as their confirmation name. 'Molaise' is not used as a personal name.[6]

Origin stories

It is usual to find some old story which supposedly explains the origin of a holy well. In the case of the well at Leighlin there are more than one. The simplest version is that the well sprang up when Laisren arrived but a more elaborate one was, about 1932, related in detail as follows by a Mrs Fitzgibbon, Rathoe National School, Tullow, and native of Leighlin:

> When St Laserian was building the cathedral of Leighlin he used bullocks for conveying the stones and other material to the site. He attached a great deal of importance to one particular bullock which was killed each evening for the suppers of the workmen, and which was alive and ready for work next morning. The workmen were warned that if a bone of the bullock was broken during the meal some great misfortune would happen to the person who broke it. One evening, whether by accident or through carelessness, a workman

broke one of the leg bones of the bullock. Next morning the saint noticed that the animal was very lame, and asked the workmen which of them broke that bone. All — including the actual culprit — denied responsibility. The saint then predicted that something very serious would happen to the person who was in [sic] fault. Next morning the guilty man found that his body was covered with painful ulcers. He went to the saint, confessed his fault and asked to be forgiven. The holy man took compassion on him, caused the well to spring up where they were standing, told him to bathe nine times in it, and assured him that the ulcers would then disappear.[7]

Such origin stories, connecting particular wells with their patron, are a common motif of holy well legends. So too are stories which explain how the well preserved itself against attempts to destroy or suppress it, moving its location as required. Thus, we find in relation to Molaise's spring at Old Leighlin that,

There is a little history attached to this well. It was not always situated where it is now. At one time it was closed by a non-Catholic and in the morning it had sprung up where it is at present.[8]

In 1782, following a visit to the cathedral of Old Leighlin, one William Domville wrote that

close by is a well sacred to the name and memory of St Lasreanus, whom the Irish call Molaisi, the waters of which well have a miraculous virtue (like the waters ordained for the Trial of Jealousy under the old law) in the finding out of truth. Insomuch that he who shall take an oath in a matter and drink these waters, if he swear falsely the water will not continue in his body and he must expect some remarkable judgement.[9]

One hundred and fifty years later one local would tell the Folklore Commission that, 'There is a tradition that anyone who has sworn falsely and drinks out of this well will have his mouth turned crooked'.[10]

Decline and dismay

If locals then and later believed in the power of the well, Domville made it clear that he personally did not and added that he would rather drink in the local tavern than partake of the waters of superstition. Others too were sceptical of the value of continuing to visit the site. By 1812 the custom of attending annually to celebrate the patron saint's feast day had been marred by unseemly behaviour on the part of some visitors. It was then proscribed by the church authorities. During the first half of the nineteenth century it was just one of many such 'patrons' to be proscribed. These had been particularly popular during the period of penal persecution when Catholics were barred from having their own chapels. As the Catholic Church recovered an institutional role in polite society, Catholic clergy grew increasingly uneasy about the annual gatherings at holy wells. They came to regard them as uncouth and scandalous.[11]

In 1795 one visitor had written that the 'famous well' at Old Leighlin 'is covered with great ash trees and much frequented by the Irish, who come to it from all parts of the kingdom'. But in 1839 it was reported to the Ordnance Survey that,

> At present the visitors of the scene are but few, the patron being prohibited since the year 1812 in consequence of the death of a man who was killed in a fray here.
>
> This was a very commendable act on the part of the parish priest of Leighlin as a greater part of the multitude who visited the place on 18 April (the Patron Day) under pretence of religious purposes, rendered it a scene of drunkenness, gambling and debauchery. Two very old ash trees and a white thorn which formerly overshadowed the well were cut down (about 1823) by the late Captain Vigors of Erindale, who leased a considerable tract of land from the See of Leighlin. The white thorn was formerly hung with all sorts of rags by the devotees, pilgrims and visitors of the holy spot. At present the well is choked up with mud and is hardly distinguishable from the marsh by which it is encompassed. About ten yards from the well stands a rude stone cross, five feet in height. The whole is surrounded by a low straggling ditch.
>
> The entire scene has one uniform appearance of desertion and desolation. There is, however, a fine prospect of the country with Mount Leinster in the distance.[12]

The writer added that the cross was 'one stone of that kind locally called fire-stone'. He included a sketch and dimensions, showing it to be the same simple cross which stands today near the well. The reference to a white thorn is not surprising as holy wells have typically had a bush or a tree growing alongside them and partaking of their sanctity. The bush most commonly associated with holy wells throughout Ireland has been the white thorn. Such bushes in Ireland and elsewhere have commonly been hung with coloured cloths and other votive offerings.[13]

In 1844 the village of Old Leighlin was said to consist, in addition to the cathedral, 'of merely the cottage of N. A. Vigors esq., and a few humble cabins'. The well was 'now almost choken up with mud and scarcely distinguishable from the expanse of marsh which surrounds it'. Certain flagstones associated with the old well appear to have been covered over. The fact that more than one spring bubbled up in the field led to some confusion. Although it was stated in 1839 that the cross was then 32 feet south of the well, Fr O'Hanlon later wrote that, 'according to popular report, St Molshi's Well, as the peasantry call it, formerly issued from beneath the base of this venerated object'. In the course of improvements made in the twentieth century the ancient cross was re-erected to the north of the well's newly arranged outflow.[14]

Revival of the well

Eventually the authorities of the Roman Catholic Church relented and once more permitted gatherings at holy wells, although these were never again as secular in their nature as they had earlier become. The site at old Leighlin was restored and solemnly blessed in 1914:

> A local farmer named James Foley suffered from a serious complaint. He made a vow that if, after bathing nine times in the well, he was cured, he would have a search made for the original well, and have it renovated. He was cured, but circumstances prevented him carrying out his vow, and he died before he could fulfil his intentions. A highly intelligent young farmer of the neighbourhood knew of Mr Foley's vow and determined to have his wishes carried out. The young man, David Murphy, was at the time (1913) captain of the local GAA [Gaelic Athletic Association] football team, and with the consent of his club organised a football tournament with the object of providing funds.[15]

A committee of prominent locals was formed and arranged for the well to be enclosed in order to preserve it. The work then carried out was described in 1934:

The enclosure, of which the walls and floor are of concrete, is about 23 feet long by 16 feet wide. The original well, which was covered with flags[tones], was found during the excavations. It is now enclosed in a concrete tank with a movable galvanised iron lid. A limestone flag in the front of the tank bears the following inscription:

A Naoimh Laisrain
Guidh Orainn.
[Saint Laisren
Pray For Us]

From the tank an overflow pipe leads into a rectangular basin which is on a lower level than the well. The water of the well is used for drinking and that of the basin for bathing affected parts of the body. The cross is inside the enclosure and is set in a concrete base....On the occasion of my visit in September 1932, there were number of Rosary beads and medals on the base of it. Outside the enclosure the whitethorn is still growing and vigorous. It is hung with medals, Rosary beads and other votive offerings, as it was generations ago. On 18 April...High Mass is celebrated in Leighlin Bridge Church. After Mass people come from the church to the well, say their prayers, drink the water, and take some of it away with them. The children of the schools have a holiday on this day. There is no formal patron: the number of votive offerings is evidence of the cures performed through the intercession of St Laserian.[16]

Modern tales

During the later 1930s, local schoolchildren participated in a national survey conducted by the Folklore Commission. A number of old stories and beliefs about the saint and his well were related by the elderly and written down by youngsters:

On that day [18 April] and for nine days after people go there to get cures for their ailments. Sore eyes, bad hearing, headaches, swollen joints, loss of appetite, all these ailments are cured if those suffering ask God through St Lazarine. This well in its own simple way is another Lourdes. It is remarkable the number of people that are cured each year.[17]

When the author visited the well in 1996 he was told by a local shopkeeper of an aunt who believed that she had been cured by the waters of the well. The shopkeeper's uncle used to walk to the well at midnight every night and drink from it before going to bed. His uncle believed that it was due to the water that he knew no illness although he lived into his eighties. He appears not to have been alone in visiting the well at midnight. Thus, in 1938 one participant in the folklore survey stated that,

> It is said that Mr Patrick Murphy, Raheenwood, was troubled with rheumatic pain. This night he went down to the well at 12 o'clock and he was on crutches. Anyone who is affected with sore eyes bathes his eyes in the water and it helps to take the soreness out of their eyes. Old people who are not able to attend [Mass?] go to the holy well and drink the water...When the people come to the well they leave crosses, coins, crucifixes. Nobody should touch those things because they apply these things to parts affected and you might take the disease. A 'sgeach' [thorn] bush grows a few yards away from the well. At this tree they leave handkerchiefs and pieces of cloth; they pray at this tree and at the holy cross they recite the rosary....The people round never use the water except there is a shortage of water....There were many cures at this well as a tree which is beside it bears many tokens such as crutches.[18]

By 1944 it was found necessary to form a new committee to take care of the well. Among its other work, the committee identified three separate springs in the field and connected these to a filter tank between the main tank and the cross. On the afternoon of 18 April 1996 the author met the last surviving member of that committee, Johnny Murphy, at his modern bungalow on a hill overlooking Old Leighlin. As we sat down to discuss the well a bright flash of lightning lit up the house and a great clap of thunder broke almost overhead. The electric doorbell then sounded twice, although there was nobody standing at the door. Then came another brilliant flash of lightning. As we stepped outside afterwards a rainbow shone over the glen towards Mount Leinster!

The work of these committees, reflecting the architectural taste of the period, served to keep the site from deterioration. Throughout the twentieth century, devout Catholics have continued to visit it. 'It is a sacred, lonely and most beautiful spot', remarked one woman in 1938. The crude stone cross, with a pierced ring and traces of roll moulding, but no inscription, stands about five feet high behind the spring.[19]

Even today, at the close of the twentieth century, this cross is festooned with votive offerings which include religious objects, batteries, toys, wedding decorations and many other knick-knacks. Nearby, pieces of cloth continued to be tied to a particular white-thorn until 1995. Then, it is said, the tree was cut away because it was rotten. This white thorn itself was a successor to that which, as we saw above, had been destroyed more than a century earlier by Captain Vigors of Erindale. It remains to be seen if this particular custom continues. In the vicinity of the well there are also personal items such as spectacles, ostensibly those of people who have been cured.

Annual celebration

On foot or by car people still make their way to the holy well of Old Leighlin, albeit now in declining numbers. They visit especially on the saint's feast-day, when a steady trickle of visitors arrives to sample and to take away the special water. Until 1998, on 18 April each year, hundreds of people gathered for Mass in the evenings. From the 1980s, in a spirit of ecumenism, they first assembled inside the Church of Ireland Cathedral. Thence, led by children who held aloft a decorated banner which bore the image of a bearded Saint Laserian, they annually made their way in procession along the roadway to the well. At the well a temporary altar was assembled under canvas.

Thus it was on the evening of 18 April 1996, when this author attended. The entrance to the field of the well was hung with green and white bunting and pansies had been planted in the ditch. A small generator powered two speakers, out of which crackled some pre-recorded old hymns. During Mass a choir of schoolchildren squeezed into the walled enclosure before the altar and sang to the accompaniment of a nun who played the electric organ. People of all ages stood around, mostly well back from the enclosure itself. The parish priest of Leighlin, Fr John Aughney, had invited Fr Michael Rodgers to concelebrate Mass. Back from an overseas posting in Africa, Fr Rodgers now works in the parish of Glendalough, Co. Wicklow, and has there rediscovered and cleaned up the neglected well of St Kevin. On that evening the gospel reading told of the woman at the well who met Jesus. During his sermon Fr Rodgers recalled a story of the origin of Leighlin's well and its association with the saint. He stated that even in pre-Christian Ireland sacred wells had 'protectors' and preached on the actual and symbolical value of the well as a source of physical and spiritual healing. Throughout the Mass the rays of the setting sun streamed through the tall spruce trees which were once imported and planted around the field, possibly in the 1940s. A fresh and pleasant breeze blew, while various birds sang and flew overhead. At the end of the ceremony the choir delivered a version of 'Hail Glorious St Patrick', adapted for 'St Laserian' with new words. Then people queued in large numbers to drink from the well, in many cases using one of the three pint glasses which were provided at the site. As the crowd of about 400 people left, members of a youth club sold copies of a magazine containing information on the history of Leighlin and other local matters.[20]

That same year there was published in Carlow a new sung-Mass in honour of 'Molaise: Saint Laserian'. In his introduction to it, the composer Liam Lawton prays, 'that as the music enfolds it will touch the Celtic psyche deep within each one'.[21]

On 18 April 1998 the traditional Mass was replaced by an ecumenical service involving both the Church of Ireland and Roman Catholic clergy. This was an historic occasion, given the bitterness which once prevailed locally between the two traditions. The service began with prayers at the Cathedral and then proceeded to the well, where this author was asked to give a short talk on the history of the local saint and did so in warm sunshine. A choir provided continuity with previous years by singing the hymn to their saint and men and women still queued to drink the water. Over 300 people attended the service.

The wells on Holy Island and at Leighlin are still respected locally and attract a new generation which is appreciative of the need for a balanced relationship with our environment.

CHAPTER 9

Remembering Laisren (Molaise)

L AISREN WAS a child of the sixth century. In his day Ireland was home to about 150 kings and their septs. Personal loyalty was owed to one's kith and kin rather than to a particular patch of soil or stretch of sea. Such social or cultural affinity as existed between septs did not amount to a sense of nationhood and various septs had their own distinct origins or origin myths. There were alliances in which a king could become the dominant overlord of a region, but there were then no centralised or national kingships of the type which developed later in Europe.

Laisren passed his earliest years between the coasts and islands of Ireland and Scotland, although no country of Scotland existed then as we now know it. At that time its northern reaches constituted the land of the Picts, while modern Ayrshire, Dumfriesshire and Galloway were home to British Celts. The highlands and islands of the west were coming to be inhabited sparsely by immigrants from Ireland, especially by the Dál Riada. Already Iona was occupied by the monks of Colum Cille, that saint who blessed the political project of Laisren's powerful grandfather, Aedán mac Gabráin.

Thus, to describe Laisren as either an 'Irishman' or a 'Scotsman', in the modern sense, is a misleading historical anachronism. One may say that he was fundamentally of Irish Celtic stock, although perhaps there was a strain of Pictish or British blood on his grand-mother's side, as we saw. The language which he spoke was the type of Gaelic which had been brought to Ireland by waves of immigrants from Europe and thence, as noted above, by the Dál Riada from north-eastern Ulster to the western parts of what later became Scotland. Indeed, we have remarked that modern Scotland owes not only a language but also its very name to the Dál Riada. For they, with other Ulaid septs, had earlier been known to the Romans of Britain as 'Scoti' and they carried that designation with them when they sailed east.

Laisren was in a position in Dál Riada to witness at close hand the ferocious and destructive competition which erupted from time to time between competing kings and their peoples. He may have perceived civilising advantages in the universalisation of Christianity, as socialists have idealistically espoused a benign world order in place of international rivalry. In any event, he committed his life to creating a substantial monastic community in the heart of Leinster, one founded on penitence and traditionally associated with healing. He is said to have presided at Leighlin over 1,500 people, an 'unusually large' number, although Bangor-on-Dee had a community of 2,000. The historical Laisren, or 'Molaise', insofar as he is known at all, was a relatively conventional if exemplary figure in the church of his era. A saint after his death, he was a busy administrator and disciplined abbot in life. He worked hard for the benefit of his contemporaries and was long warmly remembered in both Ireland and Scotland. In relation to his Leinster foundation there were celebrated,

> 300 true monks who occupied Lethglenn and 1,200 of the servants of God with Molaise and the two Ernans, and Mar[tin] holy bishop of Lethglenn.[1]

Some fifty years after Laisren's death, so we are told,

> It rained a shower of blood in Leinster this year. Butter was there also turned into lumps of gore and blood, so that it was manifest to all in general. The wolf was heard speaking with human voice, which was horrific to all.[2]

No doubt local people prayed to God for protection against such phenomena. When it came to sickness they eventually used as a charm that special litany which was associated with Leighlin:

> the seven bishops, over water against boils, and jaundice [and the plague] and every [other] pestilence. Let the water be applied to the [sick] man [*et bene sanat et reliqua. Finit. Amen. Finit*].[3]

One author, from Leighlin, has written that,

> A strong tradition regarding healing powers attributed to the monks of St Lazerian's monastery remains in the village of Old Leighlin. This healing was botanised medicines. The monks used herbs, plants, flowers and various sages. From these drinks and ointments were

concocted. It is even said that in the district round Baunree penicillin in a form was not unknown. Could it be that yesterday's superstition is today's science?[4]

The date at which the monastic community founded by Laisren ceased to function is unknown. Perhaps its members simply became the secular administrators of the new diocese founded in the twelfth century. The last person to be specifically identified as a 'successor' or coarb of Molaise of Leighlin appears to have been Conla Ua Floinn, who was noticed in the year 1113. Archdall suggests that after the Norman invasion an Augustinian cloak was thrown over many existing houses in Ireland and it is certain that an Augustinian priory was founded in the Leighlin area. Of its members we have no information and by the late fourteenth century it had ceased to exist. The earliest parts of the present church or cathedral of Old Leighlin appear to date from between 1160 and 1400.[5]

On Arran, as we saw, a site which has long been regarded as Molaise's grave was covered at some point by a decorated medieval slab It is said that about the year 1200 the lord of the isles founded 'a religious order of Molaise'. This may have been associated with that ruined 'monastery' on Holy Island about the history of which nothing is known. One eighteenth century traveller, James Robertson, thought these ruins to be 'the remains of an old chapel, built after the Gothic taste', while in the early twentieth century J. A. Balfour wrote of them that,

> Above the monastery site, built against the cliff, are some thick walls of red sandstone; what this structure can have been is difficult to determine. The remaining parts look like fifteenth or sixteenth century work.

Balfour ignored a building known variously as 'the wee house', 'boathouse' or 'old school', which stands between the burial ground and the sea and which has some appearance of a chapel. It includes worked stones which are evidently medieval and which bear some markings. It is currently in a state of poor repair.[6]

If Laisren wrote, his writings have not survived. Nor does there exist any contemporary documents referring to him. This is neither surprising nor unusual, as very few manuscripts of direct relevance to Ireland or Scotland are extant from the sixth and seventh centuries.

If we are certain that a particular person lived at a particular place then archaeology may be able to throw some light on that person's mode of living. However, in general, Laisren and his contemporaries built in wood and there are few if any structures standing from this period. Moreover, neither in Scotland nor in Ireland have the sites associated with Laisren been subjected to a thorough archaeological examination and such attention as they have received suggests that certain remains and structures are no earlier than the twelfth century, which was five hundred years after the death of Laisren in about 638.

The earliest recorded references to Laisren appear to coincide with the period when the Céli Dé flourished, between 750 and 900. The Céli Dé were tough religious reformers who preached fundamental Christianity and who practised a penitential form of self-discipline. They had great faith in the efficacy of reciting the Book of Psalms and were inspired by the example of the anchorites or 'Desert Fathers' of the Middle East and by what the Céli Dé took to be the pure and simple lives of earlier Irish saints. Their reform movement was intended to bring the church back to what they regarded as basic practices and the severity of their personal regimes, as recorded, can shock a modern reader. From accounts written during this period we learn how Laisren is said to have condemned his own sister for becoming pregnant by a monk, while at the same time he was being described as 'gentle'. Perhaps he had to be cruel to those who gave scandal in order to be kind to those who might otherwise be led astray. A later tale, from the 'Life of Maignenn', shows that Laisren subjected himself to great physical suffering in order to purge his soul of sin and guilt. The Céli Dé 'remembered' Laisren as a kindred spirit, a man after their own hearts.

However, as mentioned already, some of the old stories which show the darker and more extreme side of Laisren are not included in that extant 'Life' of the saint which survives in Brussels and which was formerly in Salamanca. This was written later than the period of the Céli Dé and appears to date from the centuries following the Norman invasion of Ireland in 1169. The present Cathedral at Leighlin was built then and the archdiocese of Dublin honoured Laisren as one of its principal saints. Pilgrims made their way across Arran to Holy Island, perhaps staying at a small monastery there. Those who wrote this 'Life', a pious medieval account of Laisren, clearly 'knew' him in their own way. The saint of the 'Life' is comfortably located in the perceived power structures of his time. Manifesting as a prodigy to his ecclesiastical uncle, he is depicted as having made his way almost casually through the monastery of his teacher and, by way of his island 'desert', on to Rome. Thence he rose to a place of prominence in the administration of the church in Ireland. Such miracles as he conducted increased his prestige and consolidated the authority of the organisation which he was helping to establish. This 'Life' represents the cult of a saint for the settled church and was just one of many pious accounts of holy men recorded by medieval scribes. However, as earlier observed, such manuscripts often included for the first time in written form tales, or versions of tales, which had been in circulation orally and they need not be dismissed simply as fanciful or credulous fabrications of their day.

The registry, records and an ancient 'Yellow Book of Leighlin', which were all still in existence at the end of the sixteenth century, may well have contained more detailed information on the saint and his legacy but they do not appear to have survived.[7]

What does still exist is a bronze matrix of the medieval seal of the cathedral chapter of Leighlin, found in a bog near Claragh, Co. Kilkenny. A version of its impression is reproduced above. This seal displays John the Baptist and a bishop – or perhaps Laisren himself as hermit and bishop. Later medieval 'arms' of the bishop of Leighlin, as published, also depict a figure which may represent 'S. Lazerianus'.[8]

The author of the pre-Reformation 'Life' of Laisren omits not only some of the older, darker stories about the saint but also any mention of Laisren's reputed role in the symbolically significant controversy which arose concerning the dating of Easter. In this context our information on him comes chiefly from a story in the medieval 'Life' of St Fintan Munnu. Its subsequent repetition in one form or another perhaps tells us more about those who have trumpeted his loyalty than it does about Laisren. Thus, in an office (form of worship) for the feast of Laisren published in Paris in 1769, it is said that, 'as legate he decreed on what day Easter should be held and got rid of disputes. He brought back to the fold all the faithful whom schism had infected/deceived'. Here was a saint for the Counter-Reformation and its aftermath, one who was said by the author of this otherwise unremarkable office to be 'shepherd of the flock', 'serious about his responsibilities' and, perhaps most appropriately in the circumstances, 'all things to all men'.[9]

However, the cult of Laisren appears to have relied for its survival as much on popular tradition as on manuscripts. In Ireland and Scotland, as we have seen, there are holy wells associated with him. It is not known when these springs were first considered blessed, there appearing to be no recorded references to them until the late eighteenth century. They may have been treated with reverence even in pre-Christian days.

At the Reformation the Church of Ireland took possession of the cathedral in Leighlin but not, apparently, of the land around the well. The latter has remained, intermittently to the present day, principally a site of Roman Catholic celebrations. It may be that the different ways in which the two traditions have tended to spell the saint's name reflected different ways in which they each wished to 'know' their patron saint. Once preferred by Protestants was 'Lazerian' and by Catholics 'Laserian', although in fact both versions were used from time to time by each tradition. Did those who in 1699, shortly after the Battle of the Boyne, designed a new crest and ordered new silver vessels for the cathedral deliberately decide to spell the saint's name with a 'zed'? This might indicate that the Laisren whom they 'knew' was a sound and sensible man, — unlike that uncouth, mystical fellow whom Catholics gathered on the marshy field of the 'well' thought that they 'knew' and whom they spelt with an 's'. There is no letter 'zed' in Gaelic. Yet, the saint now serves to bring the two churches together. In recent years the Church of Ireland authorities have made their cathedral available for Mass when the local Roman Catholic church was closed for renovations and have allowed an annual Roman Catholic procession to wend its way from inside the old cathedral up to the well. On 18 April 1998, the Church of Ireland dean even joined the Roman Catholic parish priest in an ecumenical service there. The ancient western door of the cathedral, which is little used now, faces the well and a pathway perhaps connected the two before ground levels were changed to the present arrangement.

Throughout the centuries, Laisren has been 'known' to the local people in Leighlin and Arran as 'their saint'. They may have had a more or less vague idea of what role he played in church history or what he is actually reputed to have done in life but, in any event, such information was just further proof of something which they already 'knew' about him — that he was special. They have felt that they experienced him directly at the blurred boundaries of rational knowledge. He has made their spaces sacred and is believed to have blessed their neighbourhoods with powers of healing. In some special way they have been able to connect with him through the pure spring of his well and be reassured by his imagined or experienced presence in the locality. When the old order was suppressed and their traditional way of expressing faith scorned this was a 'knowledge' with which people could contest the intellectualising of outsiders and the authority of printed books.

That their 'knowledge' of Molaise still has its own power is evident to anyone who visits Leighlin on his feast-day, when crowds gather at the well. It is also reflected in the fact that, while the name of his island was eventually displaced to the surrounding bay ('Eilean Molaise' becoming 'Lamlash'), his Scottish place of habitation came to be known simply as 'the holy isle' or, more recently, 'Holy Island'.

Today Laisren is not as widely remembered as in earlier centuries. Even the giving of his name to children around Leighlin, in the form 'Laserian', is dying out. Apart from what may be regarded as a general secularisation of Irish society, a wider sense of community has been created by modern communications and the choice of a name for a child is now made from a much broader field. To call a child 'Laserian' today is to risk having him or his parents regarded as 'old-fashioned'. It is perhaps no coincidence that the relevance of Laisren is being redefined and we are now beginning to be invited to 'know' him as a figure for our times, to locate him within a perceived tradition of 'Celtic Christianity' which is ostensibly purer than some more recent forms of institutional religion.

Like the well of Leighlin itself, 'Celtic Christianity' is regarded as a clear spring from which we can draw. In 1995, in their pastoral letter recalling the Great Famine, the Irish bishops defined penitential pilgrimages to holy wells as 'characteristic' of Irish Catholicism. It was noted earlier that on 18 April 1996 Fr Michael Rodgers, who himself has located and cleaned the overgrown well of St Kevin at Glendalough, delivered a guest sermon at Old Leighlin on the place of holy wells not only in Christian but also in pre-Christian Irish society. The site of the well at Leighlin has once more been cleaned up, its old thorn tree cut back again and locals are wondering if their village has tourist 'potential' as a place of 'heritage'. 'Heritage' is the key word in the European Union's funded policy of encouraging regions and localities to define and institutionalise their current self-image. As mentioned above, a new Mass has been composed in memory of the saint of Leighlin.

Even more fundamental is the renewed appreciation of Laisren which is evident in Scotland, where his birth name had been almost forgotten and where he is now known simply as 'Molios', 'Molio' or 'Molaise', the latter being often pronounced like 'malaise' rather than as the Gaelic 'moh-lash-eh'. Were it not for the fact that from an early date the saint's feast-day was celebrated in both places on the same date, that ancient Irish and Scottish calendars give similar information about him and that some local people have from generation to generation told the story of his arrival from and return to Ireland, one might conclude in error that the saint of Arran was not the same as the saint of Leighlin.

———————

Although the well on Holy Island has long been visited as a place of healing, there is no recent custom of celebration there each April. This may be because Arran became Presbyterian, a tradition generally hostile to the cult of saints and adverse to the celebration of feast-days, and partly because a boat ride to Holy Island in April can be considerably less attractive than a walk or a drive to Old Leighlin. Nevertheless, Holy Island retains a special place in the hearts and minds of local people, this fact being underlined both by affectionate references to it which one hears on Arran and by expressions of concern which marked its recent acquisition by a Tibetan Buddhist monastic order. There has been some anxiety that its Christian past might be disrespected or subsumed into a non-Christian 'cause'. However, Christians who in 1992 participated at Molaise's cave in an interdenominational celebration to mark the island's acquisition by Buddhists were assured that the cave and such other ancient monuments and sites as survive would be treated with respect and that the island's spiritual tradition would be kept alive and treasured.

The story of how and why Buddhists acquired the island is remarkable. It came to them from the last Duchess of Hamilton, through three intervening owners between 1958 and 1991. To the Hamiltons the holy isle had been one small portion of their immense estates, which included nearly all of Arran. If they 'knew' Molaise they did so at a distance. However, Stewart Huston, the rich Scottish-American who purchased the island from them, had a more personal interest in it. He found that it had 'the feeling of being enchanted'. A descendent of successive Presbyterian ministers at Lamlash, Huston restored the local churchyard at Kilbride and attempted to rename his property in the bay 'St Molaise Isle'. The proposal met with considerable opposition and was rejected by Arran District Council.[10]

Huston had certain remarkable ideas about the island's past. He thought that by looking sideways at the walls of Molaise's cave he got a better view of its inscriptions. This method enabled him to make out on the ceiling of the cave what he believed to be a bas relief of a naval battle, with ships of a type found in a mosaic of the port of Rome. Exploring a smaller cave near the 'monastery' he discerned what seemed to him to be a very faintly engraved form of a dancing woman, of a style which he thought to be early

Minoan, before 1600 BC. On the inside east gable end of the old 'wee house' he found a stone which apparently contained the gouged-out design of a ship, also ostensibly Minoan. While Huston appears a little too ready to jump to conclusions about Mediterranean influences, he did have a particular interest in old 'intaglios' or objects of incised design. During the period of Huston's ownership one James McCallum of Paisley investigated the historical sites on Holy Island and wrote a report on what he had found.[11]

Huston subsequently sold Holy Island to a federation of academics who wished to use it as a sanctuary for animals and whom he had permitted in 1969 to set up on it a field study centre. However, the reality of life on a western isle outweighed the imagination of those who now imported various creatures to its shores for the first time. The Universities Federation for Animal Welfare found after a decade that it could not afford to sustain its venture. So, in turn, the federation sold the island to Kay and Jim Morris. Kay had grown up in Dublin where, she says, a figure once appeared to her when she was ill and prophesied that she would come to own her own little country, 'his country'. She now concluded that the figure of her childhood experience had been Molaise and says that the moment she stepped onto Holy Island with her husband she felt that she was finally in the right place, 'his (Molaise's) country'. The couple were looking for somewhere quiet to settle after years of working in England. However, Holy Island proved to be no paradise on earth, especially in winter when the bay was rough, and Kay and Jim were themselves eventually forced to seek a buyer. Even as their second Christmas on the island approached, Kay had admitted, 'we didn't realise how hard it would be to make a living from it'. She confessed that they had been surviving on their savings: 'Now we are down to our fingernails. If we can't find a way to make an income within a year, we'll have to face the idea of selling'. They decided that farming would be impossible, being too disruptive of the environment and of the goats, ponies and other animals living on the island, and they actively considered establishing a trust,

> to be run jointly by churches in Scotland and Ireland, and to sell burial plots to people with Scottish or Irish ancestry who would like to feel a little piece of Holy Island soil is waiting for them. We've had plenty of offers to commercialise the island but we're not interested in making it into a mini-holiday camp. We've already got permission for a cemetery there and now we're talking to the churches about the idea.

If the trust is set up no one would be allowed to build on or develop on the island. It would belong to the churches and we would be its custodians. People would be able to visit their plots and to have their ashes scattered there if they wished. It would be in keeping with the sacred history of the island.

One of those with whom Kay says that she discussed the future of the island was Cardinal Tomás O Fiaich, the then Roman Catholic primate of all Ireland. However, no trust was formed and the couple did not dispose of Holy Island at that time. In 1985 Kay and her husband were reported to have proclaimed that they would give it another eighteen months to pay its way. There was talk of bottling and selling off the water from Molaise's well.[12]

When Jim's health deteriorated, it became clear that the Morris family would have to leave Holy Island. By this stage there had been three proprietors in a row motivated to buy the island because of a feeling that it was somehow enchanted or a sanctuary. Kay wished to find a fourth purchaser with a similar sensibility. Certain Tibetan Buddhists, who had come to settle in Dumfriesshire following the Chinese invasion of their homeland, were contacted by her and were receptive. They had already founded the Samye Ling Tibetan Centre at Eskdalemuir, near Lockerbie, where they were welcoming many interested visitors:

> Certainly we were not actively seeking such a property when we were approached by the island's owner Mrs Kay Morris. In the autumn of 1990, Mrs Morris wrote to Lama Yeshe Losal saying she felt slightly awkward having had for some time the wish to broach the subject of the sale of the island with us but her shyness prevented her. Finally, her circumstances were dictating that she try every possible course of action while she still had control of the situation. From the outset, Mrs Morris was aware in her own words that '*the island was using her to fulfil its destiny*'.[13]

The Tibetans were hard-pressed to raise enough money for their existing needs and ambitions and were using extensive overdraft facilities. At Samye Ling, named in memory of Tibet's oldest monastery, a temple had been constructed, opening in 1988, and there were plans for a new library and other buildings. However, Lama Yeshe accepted an invitation to visit Holy Island. While others slept he and some fellow visitors meditated and prayed, resolving to do what was possible to preserve and revitalise the place.[14]

On 21 November 1991, following several months of negotiations, a deal was signed with the Morris family and Lama Yeshe publicly confirmed his intention of purchasing Holy Island. An international appeal was launched to raise over £1,000,000, this being what it was estimated it would cost to acquire and fit out the place for the purpose of being a long-term retreat centre. The appeal was boosted by a report which was broadcast on the burgeoning international television channel, CNN, and which brought responses from as far away as Australia and South Africa. As it became clear that the Buddhists wished the property to be utilised also for inter-faith purposes, some prominent Christians welcomed their plans. The poet and monk, Dom Sylvester Houédard of Prinknash Abbey, who was a friend of the Tibetans in exile, undertook preliminary research into the Christian heritage of the island. Michael, Episcopalian bishop of St Andrews, responded positively to what he described as 'the imaginative invitation to share in the life of prayer which is planned for the island by the community of Samye Ling'. Fr Tom Connolly, press officer for the Roman Catholic church in Scotland, said that the decision to buy Holy Island made sense: 'There is great purity in the air and the inclement weather brings you closer to nature'. A writer in the *Arran Banner* referred to the island as 'Shangri-La', but some locals were cautious or suspicious, fearing the creation of a 'dependency culture' and finding the idea of such a Buddhist retreat centre 'abhorrent'.[15]

On 18 April 1992, the feast-day of St Laisren, Lama Yeshe and his colleagues took possession of Holy Island. Four days later, on Tuesday 22 April, their acquisition was celebrated by an interfaith service at Molaise's cave:

> A Roman Catholic monk stepped onto Holy Isle on Tuesday morning and fell to his knees and kissed the ground. Less demonstratively, senior Scottish clerical figures clad in cassocks and welly boots hiked up the hill to St Molaise's Cave. Other dignitaries like former Liberal leader Sir David Steel were there as well as many more, either devout or merely curious.[16]

While a Catholic monk and an Episcopalian bishop attended this service, no minister of any Arran church and no Presbyterian minister of any kind was there. The secretary for interfaith relations at the headquarters of the Church of Scotland in Edinburgh was reported to have earlier accepted an invitation to come and sent his good wishes. However, local members of the Ardrossan

Presbytery subsequently expressed reservations about the value of interfaith services, especially with non-Christians: 'I mean, who are they worshipping?', asked one. Rev. Andrew Barrie, Church of Scotland minister of the church of St Molios at Shiskine, told the author that his decision not to attend arose purely from a conceptual difficulty with interfaith worship, as Buddhists do not in fact worship God. He added that he does not think that he or his colleagues felt uneasy that Buddhists had come to own Holy Island and said that he personally has been 'treated with great courtesy' by the present owners.

For their part the invited guests who did attend were ferried to Holy Island from King's Cross, being piped ashore and met at the cave by the strains of a clarsach (Scottish harp). The piper was Mr Angus Adamson, a master of the Free Masons on Arran, who remembers the day with great warmth. The mood was described at the time by the editor of the *Arran Banner* as having been one of 'informality':

> The message was one of good will to all men (and women). Akong Rinpoche [abbot of Samye Ling] spoke first, a general talk of welcome in which he said: 'You should not worry that Tibetans are going to lock you out of Holy Isle. It was locked until we came'. Then Father Donald McGlynn, the abbot of Nunraw Abbey, spoke. He spoke of a parallel monastic tradition in Buddhism and Roman Catholicism and said: 'We are indebted to the monks of Samye Ling for bringing it (Holy Isle) to new life'.[17]

The new owners appointed a caretaker and launched a conservation programme. The first of many small waves of international volunteers began to make the short boat crossing from Lamlash to help with dry-stone walling, rhododendron clearing, tree planting and much more. The editor of the local newspaper proclaimed that the Buddhists, 'we are certain, are welcomed by the vast majority of Arran's population'. There was some local concern about rights of way and resentment at continuing restrictions on visitors, notwithstanding an assurance from the new owners that, 'anybody who would like to go to Holy Island can go by arrangement'. Specific restrictions appear to have been introduced earlier by the Universities Federation for Animal Welfare, in order to protect the island's flora and fauna in an age of growing tourism. While locals had long resorted to the island for summer picnics, the Buddhists found signs of vandalism when they first inspected the buildings on Holy Island. In practice, members of the public would not be prevented from making day-trips to the island and have continued to do so. In 1993 Jimmie Macgregor, the popular writer and broadcaster, noted that,

> Scottish opinion is divided as to whether the most recent ownership of the Holy Isle is a good thing, but the island has suffered some abuse in the past, and with the Buddhists' traditional respect for other religions and for the natural world, the place itself can only benefit from this rather strange and unexpected return to its ancient spiritual role.[18]

Buddhists, like the early Christians in Ireland, tend not to be aggressively missionary. The Buddhists of Scotland have come to 'know' Laisren as someone whom they can incorporate into their framework of reference. The Tibetan abbot of Holy Island, Lama Yeshe, has said that he will be 'more than happy [if] those with an interest in St Molaise, the cave and the tradition connected with the island' wish to rebuild what may have been a medieval place of worship at the north end of the island. He was replying to a questioner who had described that place somewhat imaginatively as 'the old Celtic chapel'. Says Lama Yeshe: 'If you are not sure about your religious practice, then there is a chance of things getting mixed together. But if you have clarity in your tradition, there is no danger in this happening'.[19]

Residents of Lamlash have become accustomed to the sight of robed Buddhists standing at the pier or walking by the sea and to a succession of television crews who wish to record what is now happening across the bay. Planning permission has been granted for a new 'centre' at the north end of Holy Island. It is intended that this building will incorporate there the old farmhouse, which is to be renovated, and that it will have forty bedrooms, as well as facilities for conferences and short retreats. It is hoped that the centre will promote peace through dialogue and that it will be open to people of all beliefs. As stated on the Internet site of the Holy Island Project,

> The Centre for Peace, Reconciliation and Retreat has been approved by the planning authorities. This will accommodate individuals and groups of all faiths and traditions. It will offer opportunities for retreat and inter-faith dialogue through meetings, conferences and workshops. The design of the Centre will be free from the signs, symbols or trappings of any particular faith.[20]

In promising to keep it 'open to all', the current owners of Holy Island may assuage the concerns of any Christians worried that the purchase of the island by Buddhists might somehow be a travesty of western traditions and beliefs. The behaviour of the Tibetans to date suggests that they understand that the island's Christian heritage is important.

Laisren's cave has a particular attraction for those who are familiar with the teachings of Tibetan Buddhists, the religious lore of the latter including many accounts of men and women who lived in caves. The practice of retreat forms a very important part of the spiritual training of their monks. Indeed it is planned to construct a private long-term retreat centre at the south end of Holy Island. This will accommodate up to 108 Buddhist monks and nuns following the three year, three month and three day retreat of the Tibetan tradition. This long-term retreat area has been designed to incorporate ecological strategies for energy, food, water and waste management. According to a current information sheet provided by the island's owners, this area will be,

> a place for deep, committed, spiritual practice. The efforts of these
> monks and nuns will bring benefit not only to themselves but will help
> preserve the transmission of the ancient wisdom of Tibetan Buddhism.
> The wealth of wisdom and understanding contained in this ancient
> lineage has already contributed much to recent developments in
> philosophy, psychology and therapy.[21]

Molaise provides an exemplary model of dedication for retreatants and the Tibetans share with many locals a sense that the island has been physically enhanced or blessed in some way by the saint's presence on it. There is also a close connection between religion and ecology in Tibetan Buddhism and the holy well or pure spring may serve as a symbol for that tradition, as it does for those who espouse 'Celtic' or 'green' Christianity. The Buddhists take special care of the flora and fauna of the island. Thus Laisren is rediscovered again as the patron of a new era.

In this age of 'cyberspace', where more appropriate to find an expression of the value of Holy Island and its traditions than on the Holy Island Project's own website?

> Celtic Christians sought the solitude of Holy Island to support their
> prayer and meditation, just as the Tibetan yogis did in the Himalayas.
> The powerful nature of these places becomes charged with the energy
> of spiritual practice which can touch the heart and inspire the mind.
> The link forged with Tibet's ancient spiritual tradition is re-awakening

Holy Island to its sacred purpose. Separated from the busy world, this sacred island will provide accommodation for both short and long retreats. It is a place to experience inner peace, to discover creativity and find meaning in this precious human life.[22]

If Laisren has been consciously 'known' and located historically, he is also 'known' in a more subtle way through symbolical association. His springs of pure water, his cave, his island, his mountain, his rock, his burial ground are all powerful images. The womb-like central location of that cave within the belly of the mountain and the issuing of a spring below its 'Judgement Stone' are particularly vibrant. Such images can open paths of communication between the self and 'otherworlds', such as are celebrated in ancient folklore and explored by modern psychology. Through this peripheral 'information' people might 'know' Laisren as a profoundly significant mediator. He is creatively suspended 'betwixt and between' their everyday reality and what lies beyond it, as he was betwixt and between wealth and poverty, between Ireland and Scotland, between Pictland and Alba, between Iona and Rome, between conservation and change, between youth and manhood, between heaven and earth. His rite of passage on a holy island was like the period which Jesus spent in the desert and it is indeed the case that such isolated places of retreat are dubbed 'disert' in Irish. You need not know many facts about such a saint to 'know' him for what he was. You expect miracles and healing and hospitality from him and, when you turn to the old accounts of his life, you find them. You 'knew' him before you knew much about him.

All of which, finally, begs a question. How does this author 'know' Laisren? Ever since first encountering the Tibetans of Scotland, initially through the pages of Thomas Merton's *Asian Journal*, I have found their example to be consoling and their quest fascinating.[23] From the moment that I heard of their interest in Holy Island, I was intrigued and stirred by the very name of that place. It excites curiosity. That someone called Molaise is said to have given up worldly power in order to live there increases one's interest. Moreover, the fact that the saint could inspire not only Christians but also Buddhists was worthy of study. Further reading and a number of visits to the Tibetan foundation of Samye Ling in Eskdalemuir have encouraged me to hope that both Christianity and Buddhism will be revitalised and the faithful heartened by contact and mutual understanding between representatives of the two religions. A greater knowledge of the history of each will facilitate cooperation.

By whatever name he is known, whether it is Laisren or Laserian, Molaise or Molios, the abbot of Leighlin and hermit of Holy Island has retained a respected place in the minds of people in both Ireland and Scotland. Notwithstanding his capacity to be very harsh on himself and on others, that being perhaps his particular human weakness, he was ultimately remembered as a 'gentle abbot'. By considering the accounts of his life we may arrive at a better understanding of the relationship between these islands off western Europe, a relationship which is intrinsically based on interdependency. Moreover, the saint's legacy provides a means whereby not only representatives of Christian churches but also members of two world faiths have been able to meet on common ground in order to worship and to celebrate in ways which express their mutual respect for each other and their commitment to the greater good. Thus does a man born nearly six centuries after Christ, a man who so served humanity that he is remembered as a saint, encourage people at the dawn of the third Christian millennium to work for the benefit of all beings.

Appendix

The saint's name

THE FORMS 'Laisren' and 'Molasse' or 'Molaise' have been adopted in the text above from the oldest manuscripts which are known to mention the saint of this study. These texts include the Calendar of Oengus and the Book of Leinster. 'Oengus' is thought to have been a monk at a monastery on the banks of the Nore. The Nore is one of the rivers which constitute 'the three sisters' of south Leinster, the others being the Suir and the Barrow. Thus, Oengus appears to have worked in the same general region as Laisren had and may well have visited his foundation. Oengus is believed to have compiled his list of saints over one thousand years ago. He wrote when the form of language which we know as 'Old Irish' was becoming 'Middle Irish'. Parts of the Book of Leinster are probably also of the same vintage as the Calendar of Oengus and most of it is not much later.[1]

The name 'Laisren' derives from the Gaelic word for 'flame', which is 'lassar', 'lassair' or 'lasair', — Welsh 'llachar'. It appears to have once been a relatively common name and was also used metaphorically of some people. Thus St Patrick, Ireland's national saint, was anciently known as 'lassar gréine ane' or 'the flame of a splendid sun'.[2] There is no reason to jump to the conclusion that the choice of this name was ever connected with sun-worship.

When the name 'Laisren' is given an affectionate twist by the prefixing of the personal possessive pronoun 'mo', meaning 'my', it becomes 'Molaise' or 'Molaisi'. The ending '-se' or '-si' is an emphatic suffix. Oengus does not appear to have used this hypocoristic form, 'Molaise', in order to designate Laisren of Leighlin, although he did use it for the two other most important saints of the same name, Laisren of Inishmurray (12 Aug.), who was the 'anam chara' or 'soul friend' of Colum Cille, and Laisren of Devenish (12 Sept.). However, both the Book of Leinster and the Lebar Brecc (c.1400), as well as later sources, refer to Laisren of Leighlin as 'Molaisi'. The earliest Scottish source, in Gaelic, also refers to 'Molaisi'. A Norwegian source of the fourteenth century has 'Malas' in connection with Holy Island. The earliest references in English to the saint of Arran are in connection with

Holy Island, which is called by Dean Monro and George Buchanan, respectively, the isle of 'Molass' or 'Molas'.[3] Rev. Andrew Barrie has told me that when in the 1980s he first came to Shiskine, on the west coast of Arran, some very elderly people occasionally referred to their saint, whom they believed to have been buried at Clauchan, as 'Moh-las', this being a trace of the Gaelic usage and language which was still heard in the district until well into the twentieth century and which is said locally to have been closer to Irish than to the Gaelic of highland Scotland.[4]

'Laisren' and 'Molaisi' are both found spelt in various ways, most of the versions being recognisably derivative. They include Laisrén, Lasrén, Lasrain, Laserian, Lazerian, Leserian, Lasrianus, Lasreanus, Laisse, Molassi, Molasius, Molingus, Molshi and Mola(i)s(s)e. Also found, usually for Laisren of Devinish, is 'Dolaise'. However, the latter saint is also known as 'Molaise' and Laisren of Leighlin himself appears in the *Cronicum Scotorum* as 'Dalaise' and 'Dolaise'! This confused Alexander Cameron.[5]

It is common for the names of medieval saints to have no single standard form of spelling. Around Leighlin today the usual form is either 'Laserian' or 'Lazerian'. The version of the medieval arms of the bishops of Leighlin which was published by Ware in 1654 and the present cathedral crest and vessels, apparently engraved in 1699, have 'z' but a stained window of 1933/4 and the exterior sign at the cathedral have 's'. Thus the use of 'z' or 's' does not necessarily distinguish Protestant from Catholic usage. 'Laserian' was once a common boy's name in Carlow but it seems to be dying out. A family complained to this author that their son was often thought by people outside Carlow to be named 'Lazarus'.

From the end of the eighteenth century, the name of the saint of Arran and Holy island is also given as 'Molio(s)', 'Maeljos', 'Mol Jos', Molise, Molees and even 'Moloi'. The form which is most commonly found on Arran today is spelt 'Molios', sometimes pronounced 'Molio'. In the case of Pennant it is clear that for him 'Maol-jos' is the saint of both Clauchan/Shiskine and Holy Island. However, some later authors, including Balfour, thought that there may have been two different saints with similar names. Their supposition appears to have been based on the differences in spellings. It is a supposition which flies in the face of a general belief on Arran that there was but one saint of Shiskine and Holy Island, a belief reflected in the existence of a 'Pilgrims' Way' connecting the two places. In fact Mackenzie, co-author with Balfour of the *Book of Arran*, seems to have satisfied himself that there was only one person involved and summarily dismissed the forms 'Molios' etc. as 'wrong etymologising'. He points out that the latter forms would derive from words meaning 'servant of Jesus'.[6]

An argument against there having been a 'St Servant of Jesus' at Clauchan is that such contrived names are not generally associated with saints of the Celtic church, although St 'Colum Cille' ('Dove of the Church') is clearly one notable exception. The church historian of Arran, J. K. Cameron, notes that 'the traditional belief is that Molash and Molios are names of one and the same person, that he carried on evangelising work both at Lamlash and Shisken and that he is buried at Cla[u]chen'. The author adds, 'It is possible that the tradition may be true, for Molash, a term of endearment, may have been the popular name of the saint, and Molios his ecclesiastical name'. The observation by Rev. Barrie, cited above, is evidence that Gaelic speakers at Shiskine used to call their local saint Molaise ('Moh-las').[7]

Clearly there is no way of answering definitively this question of whether or not there was one saint with similar derivative names or two saints with different but similar-sounding names. However, such evidence as there is points more strongly to the likelihood of one person rather than two. Even if it were somehow shown that there were two, the fact is that local people have remembered only one and certainly regard Laisren, saint of Holy Island and Ireland, as also saint of Clauchan Glen. This in itself is a tribute to his place in their hearts.

In the second volume of the *Book of Arran*, Mackenzie himself raises another hare. Having apparently rejected the possibility of a St 'Maol-jos', he suggests that the name of that saint who was believed by local people to have been buried at Shiskine was sometimes pronounced 'Bolaise' and that this may have indicated St. Blaise, in whose honour there was a chapel on Pladda Isle, off the south coast of Arran. It is difficult to see why people might have thought that an Armenian martyr was buried at Clauchan in Scotland or that the folk memory went so astray as to think that the saint of Armenia and that of Holy Island were one and the same. Perhaps Mackenzie's ear was not entirely comfortable with the local pronunciation of Gaelic.[8]

In 1807 Headrick, who had little sympathy for Gaelic culture, wrote that the name of the saint of Arran is correctly 'pronounced Molees'. This seems to correspond to no known recorded spelling. We cannot determine today how Laisren's contemporaries pronounced his name. We do know that on Arran in modern times the vowel 'a' was pronounced 'ε' and the very word taken as an example of this pronunciation by Holmer was 'las'. Thus the 'ai' in 'Laisren' might be spoken more like the 'a' in 'ash' or the 'e'

in 'hello' that the 'ai' in 'hail'. This is consistent with the most usual pronunciation of 'Molaise' in Ireland, which is 'moh-lash-eh'. The word 'mo',
meaning 'my', was originally a word separate from 'Laisren', so that pronun-
ciations which take 'Mol' as the first syllable and render it like the 'Mol' of
'Molly' seem to be wide of the mark. When the name is pronounced with
'Mol' as the first syllable and 'aise' is made to rhyme with 'maze', the result
unfortunately sounds like the French/English word 'malaise'.[9]

In 1959, when a new owner of Holy Isle proposed to change its name
to 'the Island of St Molaise', Robert McLellan presented to the Arran local
committee of Bute Co. Council a 'note on the nomenclature' of Holy
Island. McLellan, himself a local councillor as well as an author, pointed out
that the older name of Holy Isle was 'Eilean Molaise' and stated strongly that
the correct pronunciation was 'molash', with a long 'o' and a short 'a'. He
added that, 'the original Gaelic name of the Holy Isle became corrupted
partly by elision, common in the Gaelic of the south and east of Arran, and
partly from ignorance of Gaelic and of the name's meaning'.[10]

That 'Laisren' and 'Molaise' were common names in Celtic Ireland may
be seen from an inspection of the Book of Leinster and other manuscripts.
Over a dozen men and women with names based on the root 'las-' were
regarded as blessed or saintly by the medieval church. The men included
Laisrean, son of Feredach, Abbot of Iona, and Laisrén of Devinish, an island on
Lough Erne (12 Sept. Died 563. Plummer's 'Life of Molaise' is about this saint). The
female version of the name was Las(s)air or La(i)sse, Latinised as Lassara or
Lasrea. O'Hanlon counted in the Martyrology of Donegal no less than
fourteen distinct entries of holy women so named. An old Irish 'Life' of one
of these saints, whose feast-day falls on 13 November, has been published.[11]

References

Introduction

1. *Book of Clanranald*, pp 156-7.

2. *LL (Book of Leinster)*, col. 372b; *Martyrology of Oengus*, pp 107, 127; *Martyrology of Gorman*, p.79.

3. Vita S. Lasriani seu Molaisse, abbatis de Lethglenn (Bibliothèque Royale, Brussels MS), printed in Heist, *Vitae Sanctorum Hiberniae*, pp 340-3; Kenney, *Sources*, p.451 who considers this 'Life' to be 'late and unsatisfactory'; Sharpe, *Medieval Irish saints*, pp 376-7, 380-81, 395. The details in the two later texts generally coincide with those in the Salamanca manuscript. However, where it is missing a page, they provide additional information. One of the two later texts is a manuscript kept in Maynooth, Co. Kildare, and the other appears in a book published in the seventeenth century. Both of these versions were copied from earlier manuscripts which are thought to have been lost. The Maynooth text was penned in 1627 by Thomas Arthur, philosopher and doctor of medicine, who copied certain pages in the library of Dr James Ussher. The text published in a book was copied from a manuscript which was then in the possession of a Jesuit priest, Henry Fitzsimon, from whom it takes its name (A collection of lives of Irish saints, in Latin (St. Patrick's College, Maynooth, MS) contains the Arthur MS; *Acta S.S.*, 18 April, for the Latin text of Fitzsimon's manuscript, 'De S. Lasreano sive Molassio'. A translation of this into French by François Chenique, made 18 April 1991, was helpful to me (Samye Ling MS)).

4. For a discussion of the significance of such accounts see Heffernan, *Sacred biography* and a review of this by Thomas Clancy in *The Innes Review*, xlvi, no. 2 (Autumn, 1995).

5. Mark Rowe in *Independent on Sunday*, 15 Feb. 1998.

1: Royal blood

1. Byrne, *Irish kings and high-kings*, pp 8-11, 106-7.

2. McLellan, *Monuments of Arran*, p.7; *Place-names of Scotland, passim*.

3. *LL (Book of Leinster)*, col. 372b; *Book of Leinster*, p.1693. For 'Monadh' see Reeves, *Life of Columba*, pp 201, 377, 437n; *Celtic place-names*, pp 391-6; Wainright, *Picts*, p.149. Behind Lamlash, Arran, is a 'Monadh Mór'.

4. Dillon and Chadwick, *Celtic realms*, pp 69-70; Shaw, *Men of the north*, p.230, citing the complex Book of Ballymote which has never been fully translated or indexed. Shaw gives no specific reference.

5. Byrne, *Irish kings*, pp 109-10, 285; *Book of Leinster*, p.1155 gives 'Mo Lasse Lethglinn, m[ac] Cairell Chruaid...', the latter epithet perhaps indicating that Cairell was regarded as 'stern' or 'harsh'. It continues '...m[ac] Muredaig, mac Fhorgo'. See also *Book of Leinster*, p. 1705 (*LL [Book of Leinster]*, col. 374e).

6. *Celtic place-names*, p.192; Dillon and Chadwick, *Celtic realms*, pp 19-21, 50, 175; Thomas, *Britain and Ireland in early Christian times*, pp 56-62 ('Irishmen in Man and Wales'); Dillon, 'Irish settlements in Wales', pp 1-12.

7. Skene, *Coronation stone*, pp 18, 44 contradicts the legend; Morris, *Age of Arthur*, p.180; Chadwick, *Celtic Britain*, p. 60; Dillon and Chadwick, *Celtic Realms*, p.69; McLellan, *Monuments of Arran*, p.7; Anderson, *Sources*, i, 1-12; Hudson, *Kings of Celtic Scotland*, pp 2-3; For Dunadd, in the parish of Glassary, county of Argyll, see Lane, 'Some Pictish problems at Dunadd' in Friell and Watson, *Pictish studies*, pp 43-64. Today, small craft may get through from Crinan Bay to ancient Dunadd at abnormally high tides. It is not known if a waterway was once kept open permanently (MacDonald, *Argyll*, p.19).

8. F. J. Byrne in *N.H.I.*, ii, 18-19.

9. Mac Neill, *Phases of Irish history*, pp 194-200; Chadwick, *Early Scotland*, ch. ix, 'The kingdom of Dalriada'; Bannerman, *History of Dalriada*, pp 81-90.

10. Smyth, *Celtic Leinster*, pp 78-83, 133, who includes details of an impressive web of intermarriage in Leinster, notwithstanding recurrent internecine strife between its kings. Duncan says that one of Aedán's sons, Gartnait, became a king of the Picts, 'implying a Pictish mother'. Among the Picts a man became king through his mother and was succeeded not by his son but by his mother's son (brother) or by his mother's daughter's son (his nephew). For this matrilineal system see Wainright, who adds that 'the fathers of other Pictish kings seem to have been Scots from Dál Riada'. Gemma is said in the Salamanca manuscript (S.1) to have been the niece of a British king. Bannerman deduces from this that her mother was also British, which if true does not necessarily exclude Duncan's proposition that Aedán had a relationship with a Pictish princess. Indeed, if Gemma's uncle was British then it might not be that her father married a British woman but that some paternal aunt married a Briton. Moreover, mortality may account for a man being married twice but it is also the case that in the sixth century monogamy was by no means strictly required of Gaelic kings. Such factors complicate efforts to discover who was related to whom (Bannerman, *History of Dalriada*, pp 86, 88-91; Duncan, *Scotland*, pp 42-46; Wainright, *The Picts*, pp 25-28); Chadwick, *Early Scotland*, pp 90-91.

11. Byrne, *Irish kings*, p.95; Byrne, *Celts*, p.159.

12. Richter, *Medieval Ireland*, pp 54-56; *Encyclopaedia of Irish folk tradition*, pp 92-96.

13. Scott, 'St Maolrubha', pp 262-3; Byrne, 'The island of St Columba', pp 37-58. There is a legend that Aedán's father was buried on Iona. Reeves, *Columba*, pp 417-8 describes this as 'one of the anachronisms so frequent in Scottish hagiography', but is it possible that Colum chose Iona because there was already a pre-Christian burial site there? Certainly the descendants of Aedán are believed to be interred on the island.

14. Bannerman, *History of Dalriada*, p.82.

15. *Adomnán's Life of Columba*, pp 32, 189-90.

16. Reeves, *Life of Columba*, pp 433-6; Chadwick, *Celtic Britain*, p.60; Dillon and Chadwick, *Celtic Realms* , p.182; Shaw, *Men of the north*, pp 229-32. A recent study of one of Colum Cille's prophesies suggests that aspects of Dál Riadan affairs which displeased church historians were unlikely to find their way into monastic annals (Picard, 'The strange death of Guaire Mac Aedáin', pp 367-75).

17. Bannerman, *History of Dalriada*, pp 157-70. The encounter at Mag Roth is said to have been decisive for Suibhne, one of the most intriguing figures in Irish literature. He became 'geilt' and subsequently led his life wandering amongst trees and eating herbs and wild grasses. Warriors might become 'geilt' or 'volatiles' owing to their looking up into the sky during fighting and suddenly realising the horror of slaughter. Suibhne was possibly a king of the Dál Riada or of the Dál nAraide, another Ulaid sept. He was later befriended by St Moling of Carlow who, as we shall see, is said to have known Laisren. Some have found in Suibhne a parallel to or identification with the Arthurian Merlin (Chadwick, *Saints in the early Celtic church*, pp 105-7; Jackson, 'The story of Suibhne Geilt', p.540; Byrne, *Kings*, pp 110-111; Bannerman, *History of Dalriada*, pp 82-3; Nagy, 'The wisdom of the geilt', pp 44-61; Nagy, *Buile Suibhne, passim*; Carey, 'Suibhne Geilt and Túan Mac Cairill', pp 93-7).

18. Healy, *Ireland's ancient saints and scholars* , p.322 for a usual version of the legend. Colum Cille was certainly popular enough with the poets to be commemorated in the *Amra Coluim Chille*, which is believed to be the most ancient surviving poem in Old Irish.

19. Carney, *Studies in Irish literature*, pp 262-6; MacCana, *Celtic Mythology*, p.15; *Encyclopaedia of Irish folk tradition*, pp 364-69; Richter, *Medieval Ireland*, pp 12, 56, 138.

20. *Thes. Pal.*, ii, 310; Moran, 'Early Irish missionaries in Britain', pp 168-200 and 328-92 for Scotland; Dillon and Chadwick, *Celtic realms*, pp 76, 182; Campbell,

'A cross-marked quern from Dunadd and other evidence for relations between Dunadd and Iona', pp 105-17; Anderson, 'Lists of kings', p.108; Williams, *Lords of the isles*, ch. 5. Twenty miles west of Lewis there is also a small group known as 'The Flannan, Seven Hunters or Holy Isles' (*S.H.R.*, ix [1912], p.107). The Dál Riada may also have brought the ogham alphabet, of which there is a sample in the King's Cave, Arran (Thompson, *Gaelic Scotland*, p.220). A view once held by some British writers that the Scoti were earlier driven from Scotland by the Picts, only to return subsequently to their homeland, is considered uninformed today.

2: Miracle-worker and migrant

1. Chadwick, *Saints in the early Celtic church,* pp 102-3. Adomnán does not refer to Molaise of Arran and Leighlin. It is equally possible that Laisren was named after the saint of Devenish in Fermanagh, who died in 563.

2. *Orig. Paroch.*, p.246; *Celtic place-names*, pp 37-8; *Calendar of Oengus*, p. cxxx gives 'Bláán of fair Cenngarad', to which later scribes have added, 'i.e. Dumblane his chief city and of Cenngarad is he, i.e. in Galloway'. The 'Lives' do not specify on which side of Laisren's family it was that Blaan was his 'uncle'. Sometimes Rathlin Island was also included as part of an Arran group. It was not necessary for sailors to round Kintyre to go from Arran and Bute to Islay. There are narrow flat sands joining Kintyre and Knapdale, across which 'birlings' and other boats, some up to ten tons, have been drawn by men and horses from coast to coast. Plans to cut a channel here were overtaken by the opening of the Crinan Canal further north. It was practice for early seamen to disembark and to cross even greater promontories to avoid stormy waters (Buchanan, *History of Scotland*, p.17; Thompson, *Highlands and islands*, p.196; Bowen, *Saints, seaways and settlements*, pp 3, 18).

3. *Synod of Argyll*, i, 252 for Eilean Munde; Elen-Mun; Isle of Munnu; Plummer, *Vitae SS Hib.*, i, lxxxiv, who notes that Munnu was reputed to have Druidic associations; Knight, *Early Christianising of Scotland*, pp 127-8; Baring-Gould, *Lives of the saints*, at 21 Oct. (Fintan Munnu). Arthur gives 'Murin' instead of 'Mundus'.

4. *Encyclopaedia of Irish folk tradition*, p.46.

5. Chadwick, *Saints in the early Celtic church* , pp 82-5, 101-5 for quotation; Dillon and Chadwick, *Celtic realms*, pp 178-9; Stokes, 'Island monasteries of Wales and Ireland', pp 658-664; Mackinlay, '"*In Oceana Desertum*" — Celtic anchorites and their island retreats', pp 129-33; McRoberts, 'Hermits in medieval Scotland', p.200; Cowan and Easson, *Med. religious houses*, p.235; Charles-Edwards, 'Irish *peregrinatio*', pp 43-59.

6. Anon., 'The green island', p.191; O'Rahilly, 'The names Érain and Ériu', pp 1-28; Dillon and Chadwick, *Celtic realms*, p.135.

7. Duncan, *Scotland*, p.5. For an overview of the physical remains of successive waves of invasion and settlement see generally *Book of Arran*, i.

8. *Celtic place-names*, pp 63 (citing 'Book of Ballymote'), 65-7, 87, 96-7; MacCana, *Celtic mythology*, pp 69-73; O'Rahilly, *Early Irish history and mythology*, pp 142, 145; Dillon and Chadwick, *Celtic realms*, p.147; Morris, *Age of Arthur*, pp 116-19; O Cuív, 'A poem in praise of Raghnall', pp 297-8.

9. 'Agallamh na senórach' at *Silva Gadelica*, i, 102 & ii, viii, x-xi, 109. Arran folklore has it that Oisín, son of Fionn, died and was buried on the island.

10. Byrne, *Celts*, p.77, notes that after the ninth century the term 'Alba' changed from signifying 'Britain — the classical Albion' to denote the territories of the Dál Riada/Scoti and their Pictish or 'Cruithen' allies, a confusing transformation. The words 'idir Albain ocus Cruithentua[i]th' thus seem to indicate an early date of composition for the passage just quoted. They are, in any event, inadequately translated as 'betwixt Scotland and Pictland' and better might be, 'betwixt the territory of the Britons and that of the Picts'. By the same token the Fitzsimon manuscript seems to be late. The Salamanca version omits any reference to either 'Alba' or 'Picts'.

11. Meyer, *Ancient Irish poetry*, p.59.

12. McLellan, *Isle of Arran*, p.72; Fairhurst, *Arran's past* (ed. 1982), p.53; Sharp, 'Arran', pp 205-8.

13. Map of Buteshire in *N.S.A.*, v (1845), v, 52; *Book of Arran*, ii, 263; Hall, *South Arran*, p.38 shows a family, perhaps gypsies or travellers, 'living in the Monster or Black Cave' on Arran.

14. Martin, *Western isles*, p.220; Headrick, *Arran*, p.388.

15. *N.S.A.*, v 24; Campbell, *West highlands*, i, 75; Stokes, 'The death of the sons of Uisneach', pp 127 (where 'Dún Fiodh' is given also with 'Dún-finn'), 145, 172; Gemmell, *Discovering Arran*, pp 55, 152 for Dún Fionn today.

16. *Encyclopaedia of Irish folk tradition*, pp 301-3; Dillon and Chadwick, *Celtic realms*, pp 151-2.

3: The holy isle

1. Stokes, *Life of Patrick*, pp 162f., 168f; Chadwick, *Early Scotland*, p.123; , Dillon and Chadwick, *Celtic realms*, p.69; Bieler, *Christianisation of the insular Celts*, pp 116-7 for a similar lack of information on the Christianisation of Man.

2. *Book of Arran*, i, 154; Cameron, *Church in Arran*, p.35; Reeves, *Life of St Columba*, pp lx-lxvii; Burleigh, *Church history of Scotland*, p.19; Grinsell, *Folklore of pre-historic sites in Britain*, pp 230-321.

3. Pennant, *Scotland*, p.188. The Latin might be translated as, 'Here an island makes the harbour, its cliffs a shelter'.

4. Kerr-Hunter, 'Holy Isle', p.31. Mullach Mór is 1,026ft/314m feet high.

5. *Carmina Gadelica*, i, 326; ibid., ii, 328-9; 'Ch. II, Taking of evidence in Scotland, p.87' (Holy Island boxes, Samye Ling, photocopy of unidentified text). The word 'fairy' has certain modern sentimental connotations. Such spirits were believed to live in knolls and hills and were known in Gaelic to the people of Arran as 'sifri', 'sith', 'sithich', 'sibhridh' or 'sithichean' (*Carmina Gadelica*, ii, 326-9; *Book of Arran*, ii, 254-72).

6. *Carmina Gadelica*, ii, 328-9; Wilson, *Annals of Scotland*, pp 89-90; *Arran Banner*, 2 and 23 Nov. 1991; Cowley, *Annals of Arran* (1992), col. 118.

7. Kerr-Hunter, 'Holy Isle', p.32; *The Times*, 8 Feb. 1992, citing Lama Yeshe, a Tibetan Buddhist monk who himself has spent twelve years in retreat and who is executive director of the Holy Island project and retreat-master of Holy Island. He recently completed a 49 day dark retreat on Holy Island.

8. Headrick, *Arran*, pp 80-81.

9. Bremner, *Norsemen in Alban*, pp 250-51; Duncan, *Scotland*, pp 578-9; Barrow, *Kingship and unity*, pp 109-12; Anderson, *Sources*, ii, 608-42; Wilson, 'Holy island and the runic inscriptions of St Molio's Cave', pp 45-56; Roger, 'Notes on two additional runic ristings in St Molio's Cave', pp 378-80; Balfour, *Book of Arran*, i, 23; Olsen, 'Runic inscriptions', p.169; Liestol, 'Rune', p.237. Casts of four of these runic inscriptions are kept at the National Museum of Scotland, Edinburgh (cat. nos 293-6).

10. Balfour published his findings in the *Book of Arran* and in Balfour, 'Ecclesiastical remains in the Holy Island'. In 1970 further excavations were carried out at the cave ('Excavations in the cave of Saint Molaise and at other sites on Holy Island by Dr James D. P. McCallum' (Isle of Arran Museum MS 277)). It is desirable that professional archaeologists conduct a thorough examination of all historic sites on Holy Island before irreparable harm is done by amateur investigations or planting and building. There are carvings in at least two other caves on Holy Island. Over that of Molaise Firsoff saw what 'could resemble' a boat with a man in it (*Arran with camera and sketchbook*, pp 81-6).

11. Kerr-Hunter, 'Holy Isle', p.32 who adds, 'I have had many blessings'; Chadwick, *Saints in the early Celtic Church*, pp 103-4. When visiting Molaise's cave in the summer of 1960, Stewart Huston had his attention called to the noise of running water, which he thought suggested that there might be an early well or spring even closer to the cave than is the visible spring (Cowley MS: Huston

to Laidlaw). Local people still visit the cave and well for religious reasons and even some Presbyterians drink the holy water: 'Why not?', one asked. It is not known how another spring, on the south-east coast of Holy Island, became known as 'Dorothy's Well'.

12. *Book of Arran*, i, 259, 298-9; Historic Scotland (Edinburgh) MS, NS 02 NE 6: File notes; Knight, *St Molios*, p.9; *Supernatural Arran*, cols 33-4 where Cowley also notes that at Sannox a certain rocking stone is said to have been used as a place of final appeal in difficult legal cases. Auchencairn is not far from Lamlash Bay. Under 'cutty stool' the *O.E.D.* gives 'Formerly in Scotland, a particular seat in a church, where offenders against chastity, or other delinquents, had to sit during the time of divine service and receive a public rebuke from the minister; the stool of repentance'. The editor of the *O.E.D.* cites Newte, *Tour Eng. & Scot.* (1791): 'In most of the kirks there is a small gallery...painted black, placed in an elevated situation, next the roof of the church, which they call the cutty stool, and on which offenders against chastity are forced to sit'.

13. Balfour, 'Ecclesiastical remains', pp 157-8; Historic Scotland (Edinburgh) MS, NS 02 NE 6: File notes.

14. Martin, *Western isles of Scotland*, pp 225-6.

15. Ibid., Heraughty, *Inishmurray*, p.29. The island of Inishmurray was home to that Molaise who was the 'anam chara' of Colum Cille.

16. *N. S. A.*, v, 24.

17. Smith, *Life of Columba*, pp 22-3n; *Book of Arran*, i, 272; ibid., ii, 309; Macphail, 'The cleansing of I-colum-cille', p.17; Brenneman, *Holy wells of Ireland*, pp 13-14, 37, 40, 44, 58-61, 64. The figure of over 3,000 wells is given also at Lucas, 'Sacred trees', p.40. In 1891 an ancient stone ball, said to be one of nearly 400 found in Scotland ('and nowhere else'?!) was discovered at Dippin on Arran and has since been presented to the Museum (Fairhurst, *Arran's past* (ed. 1988), pp 23-4, including a sketch of the Dippin stone; *Annals of Arran* (1992), col. 115).

18. *Ériu*, i (1904), p.39; ibid., ii (1905), pp 55-57; Meyer, *Ancient Irish poetry*, pp 30-31; Murphy, *Early Irish lyrics*, p.28, no. 9. The poem is not later than the ninth century.

19. Monro, *Western Isles*, p.486; Headrick, *Arran*, p.81; *N.S.A.*, v, 25; Balfour, 'Ecclesiastical remains in the Holy Island', 147-58; Kerr-Hunter, 'Holy Isle', p.32; Kersley Holmes, 'Holy Island'; Huston to Laidlaw (Cowley MS); Pennant, *Scotland*, p.162; *Supernatural Arran*, col. 38 for the *Madadh Alluidh* or *Madadh Fuil* ('wild-wolf' or 'blood-dog'). *Gaelic Dict.* gives 'madadh' as 'the usual term in Arran for a dog, where cú is seldom heard'. Cf. Irish 'madra'.

20. *N.S.A.*., v, 25; McArthur, *Antiquities of Arran*, p.164; *Annals of Arran* (1992), col. 91 suggests that the 'perpetrator' died before his first crop was ready to be gathered.

21. Landsborough, 'A sculptured cross', pp 74-7. The author adds that two cruciform headstones were also found, within the chapel at Kilbride: 'one still there; the other now placed over the grave of a sailor-boy, whose body was washed ashore in Lamlash Bay'. Beside the cross in Lamlash is an object which resembles a medieval mortar and which some locals also believe may have been on Holy Island, where it possibly served as a holy-water font (Balfour, 'Ecclesiastical remains on the Holy Isle', pp 148-9; *Book of Arran*, i, 224, 229-31 (incl. plate of floral cross at Clauchan), 257-60; Fairhurst, *Arran's past* (ed. 1982), pp 91-92; *Annals of Arran* (1992), cols 91, 111 (giving 1884-6 as the date of the new Kilbride Church, Lamlash), 115). See also ch. 7, note 20, below.

22. *Book of Arran*, i, 224, 257-60; Partial survey of Holy Island, 1994 (GUARD MS). In 1983 Margaret Fagg, whose grandmother was born on and married from Holy Island, recalled mention of 'a stone — or would it be slate? — coffin. The trees at the back of the house, beyond the house, the place was called "The Monastery"'. Her grandmother was one of the McIntyres who had long been tenants of the island and 'for many years until the monastery cottage fell into ruins all the family came back for holidays'. They had '"the let" of a cottage near the shore....The Island has always had a charm for the families scattered over the world, and they make for its shores, when possible, to feel its peace and solace' (Margaret Fagg, née Paterson, to Isle of Arran Museum, 1983 (I. O. A. Museum archive)).

23. Cameron, *Church in Arran*, p.30; Boyd-Scott, *East of Arran* p.52; Cowley to this author, 31 Oct. 1996. *Place-names of Arran* gives the process of transition as: 'Eilean Molaisi — Elmolaisi-Lamolash-Lamlash'. There is documentary evidence from the fourteenth to the seventeenth century of its developing use in the forms Almelasche or Almeslach, Malas-ey ('ey' is 'isle'. E.g. 'ey-O'/Io/Iona), Helantinlaysche, Mallanche, Molass, 'Island Molas i.e. Lamlach or Lamlash', Lamlach, Lamlash. A reference by Munro suggests that Lamlash Bay was earlier known as 'the ness of Kilbride' (*Misc. Scot.*, ii, 114-5, 176; Fordun, i, 13 and ii, 39). Kersley Holmes, 'Holy Isle', alone challenges any assumption that 'Holy' in 'Holy Island' refers to the sanctity of Molaise. The truth, he claims, is that 'Holy' is somehow a corruption of two Gaelic words which he gives as 'oil-e' and which he believes designate an 'island of instruction'. Steve Blamires alone suggests that an old name for Holy Island was 'Inis Shroin', which he translates as 'Island of the water spirit' (*Holy Island Project Newsletter* (1993), p.17). His unreferenced suggestion has been repeated subsequently but must be treated with caution. The Irish word 'srón' refers to a

projection in general and a nose in particular and if Holy Island was ever 'Inis Shroin' then this was possibly a reference to its appearance.

24. Headrick, *Arran*, p.81. Headrick apparently believed that the geological knowledge of his day was literally consistent with the account of creation in the Bible (*Arran book file*, col. 14).

25. *Carmina Gadelica*, i, 326; Hall, *Isle of Arran*, p. 52; McRoberts, 'Hermits', p.201; Richards, 'Early Welsh church', pp 337-8; Smyth, *Celtic Leinster*, p.29.

26. Cameron, *Church in Arran*, p.17; *Supernatural Arran*, col. 33.

27. Headrick, *Arran*, pp 8-9; *N.S.A.*, v, 24, says 'Molios...was a disciple of St Columba'. Headrick describes Eilean nam Ban (The Women's Isle) in the sound of Iona, where Columcille is said to have sent the nuns of Iona (Martin, *Western isles*, pp 264-5), as a 'seraglio' (harem) and raises the possibility that the strange death of Oran on Iona was murder. Headrick purports to rely on Smith's *Life of Columba*, which provides no basis for his more extravagant remarks. However, see Reeves, *Columba*, pp 203-4, 417-8.

28. Macdonald and Macleod, *Gold key and green life*, pp 190-214; Sharp, 'Arran', p.205.

29. Knight, *Early Christianising of Scotland*, ii, 129.

30. Boyd Scott, *East of Arran*, pp 9-10, 67-88. Kerr-Hunter, *Holy Isle*, p.32 tells the story of how Molaise supposedly routed and converted 'a colony of Vikings in the Monamore Glen', its members having become abusive. This was quite an achievement as the first Viking raid on Scotland took place two centuries after the saint lived.

31. *Thes. Pal.*, ii, 296; Meyer, *Ancient Irish poetry*, p.100.

4: Via Rome to Leinster

1. There are vague reports of the finding of three Roman coins on Holy Island and some of those baptised on Arran in the seventeenth century ostensibly had Roman names such as Aeneas and Gillatius. Of course any such coins or descendants of Romans may have come to Arran long after the decline of Roman Britain (Ruddock, 'Those were the days'. p.12; Bateson, 'Roman coins', p.168; Giblin, *Irish Franciscan mission to Scotland*, pp 39-40).

2. Lanigan, *Ecclesiastical history of Ireland*, ii, 384, 402-3. Perhaps the number 'fourteen' (Latin: *quatuordecim*) arises in connection with the '*Quartadecimans*' heresy which was associated with the dispute over Easter in which Laisren took Rome's side, as we shall see. Unfortunately I have elsewhere repeated the figure of fourteen without question (O'Hanlon, *Lives*, iv, 210, n.4; Kenny, *Kilmainham*, p.16).

3. Mac Neill, *Lughnasa*, p.168 citing Shirley, *Farney*, p.159 and Shirley, *Monaghan*, p.519. But also note ch.6, n.9 below. See appendix for 'Laisren' and 'Lasair'.

4. Kenny, *Kilmainham*, p.24, n.6.

5. Byrne, *Kings*, pp 130-1.

6. For sagas relating to Dinn Ríg see O'Curry, *MS materials*, p.252; Smyth, *Celtic Leinster*, pp 7-8, 117 (citing *Book of Lecan*, facsimile 194.a.1) and especially p.127, n.2; Orpen, 'Motes and Norman castles', pp 245-7 quotes Keating who wrote that Dinn Ríg was 'on the bank of the Barrow between Carlow and Leighlin, on the west side of the river' (Keating, *Foras feasa*, i, 31). The Anglo-Norman settlement of New Leighlin was centred on Burgage, to the south of Ballyknockan Mote. A fragment of the Annals of Tigernach at Rawlinson 502, f.1, b, col. 1 states that Dinn Ríg is in Mag-Ailbe, for which see ch. 6 below (*A.F.M.*, a.m. 3267, 4658).

7. Dillon, 'Consecration of Irish kings', p.6; Byrne *Kings*, pp 132-3; Smyth, *Celtic Leinster*, p.76; Laing and Laing, 'Scottish and Irish metalwork', pp 211-21. Mobility was more common in early times than is sometimes supposed. Thus, Laisren's father's sept, the Dál Fiatach of Co. Down, are credited with a Munster origin while Cairbre Rigfhota, the ancestor of his mother's sept, the Dál Riada, is said to have settled in Munster (O'Rahilly, 'The names Érain and Ériu', p.7, notes).

8. Ware, 'Bishops', p.23; Meyer, 'Early relations between Gael and Brython', p.39; Bannerman, *History of Dalriada*, p.90; Bowen, *Saints, seaways and settlements*, p.3; Moore, *The Irish sea province*, pp 1-86; *Adomnán's Life of Columba*, pp 212, 490; Stokes, 'Island monasteries', p.660; MacNeill, *Lughnasa*, p.342.

9. Brooks, *Knights fees*, p.56 notes that even as late as the twelfth century 'Obargy included the present barony of Slievemargy, Leix, and parts of Co. Carlow, in the baronies of Carlow and Idrone West'; Smyth, *Celtic Leinster*, pp 9, 59-61, 65, 82. Harbison, *High Crosses*, p.377 notices that a panel of the high cross at Moone is paralleled in Scotland at Dunkeld, but thinks that this is 'scarcely likely to be earlier than the middle of the eight century'.

10. Smyth, *Celtic Leinster*, pp 77, 81-2; Byrne, *Celts*, p.106; Plummer, *Vitae SS Hib.*, ii, 16; Flower, *The Irish Tradition*, pp 22-3.

11. Plummer, *Vitae SS Hib.*, ii, 16; O'Hanlon, *Saints*, v (10 May for Comghall); Baring-Gould, *Lives of the saints*, at 10 May and 21 Oct. (Fintan Munnu); Flower, *The Irish tradition*, p.29; Smyth, *Celtic Leinster*, pp 77, 94 and 91 where the author warns of making too much of the tribal origins of saints, 'since they were clearly free to move across tribal boundaries in somewhat the same way as

entertainers and the learned classes'. Scott, 'St Maolrubha', p.262 notes that St Maolrubha, who worked among the Picts and founded a monastic settlement at Applecross, was a grand-nephew of Comghall.

12. Bannerman, *History of Dalriada*, pp 89-90, who adds that 'Echtra Aedán mic Gabráin' is the title of the prose tale, now lost, which occurs in the saga list of the Book of Leinster.

13. O'Brien, 'Middle-Irish poem on the birth of Aedán Mac Gabráin and Brandub Mac Echach', pp 157-70.

14. Bannerman, *History of Dalriada*, pp 89-90.

15. Curry, *Battle of Magh Leana*, p.96; Jackson, *Cath Maighe Léne*, p.102; Hayden, 'District of Leighlin', pp 4-6; Anon., 'The episcopal village of Old Leighlin' (an undated local leaflet); Local verbal accounts.

16. *Rennes Dindsenchas*, xv, pp 277-79. The term 'brosna suad' is given by him as 'faggot (?) of sages', 'faggot' being a bundle of sticks, usually intended for fuel. His question mark is not so much directed at the word 'brosna' as at this particular epithet. Dineen indicates that it was a technical term used by the poets to indicate a type of verse (Dineen, p.129).

17. Lucas, 'Sacred trees of Ireland', pp 16-17, 20. See *LL (Book of Leinster)*, col. 199b 61 et seq; Milner, *Tree book*, pp 80-84 for ancient yews, some said to be thousands of years old and 'many' associated with ancient burial sites. The 'villy' of 'Rathvilly', in Co. Carlow, is generally thought to be from 'bile' (*Place-names of Ireland* and *Place-names of Carlow, passim*).

18. Mac Cana, *Celtic mythology*, p.50.

5. Settled in the half-glen

1. *LL (Book of Leinster)*, col. 372b; *Book of Leinster*, vi, p.1693; *Martyrology of Oengus*, pp 107, 116-7; Smyth, *Celtic Leinster*, p.102.

2. *Arch inv. Carlow*, pp 9, 69; *Account roll of the priory of the Holy Trinity Dublin*, pp 106, 181; In the east of Carlow, below Mount Leinster, is also a cairn of Raheenkyle, the ending '-een' being the diminutive 'ín' or 'little' in Irish. There are Rathcool(e)s in, for example, counties Cork, Dublin, Kilkenny and Tipperary, a Raghill in Wexford, Rathkeil in Fermanagh and Rathkyles in Kilkenny and Wexford. Fionn's father was reputed to have a mansion at Raith Cumhaill, otherwise Rathcoole, Co. Dublin (Curry, *Cath Magh Lene*, p. xi). Oisín was associated with another Rathcol, a little to the east of Stranraer by the Bay of Luce in Galloway. This was on one of the promontory crossings of early seamen going from the Firth of Clyde to Ireland (Hogan, *Onomasticon*,

pp 333-8; Waddell, *Ossian and the Clyde: Fingal in Ireland*, p.177; Bowen, *Saints, seaways and settlements*, p.18).

3. U.C.D. Folklore MS 907. For a picture of this St Patrick's Well, said to be visited chiefly for curing warts, see *Arch. inv. Carlow*, pp 74, 76; Smyth, *Celtic Leinster*, pp 9, 20, 32 says Iserninus was based at Toicuile in Clíu: 'We cannot identify Toicuile but clearly the first element Toi represents Welsh *ty* rather than old Irish *tech*'; *O.S. letters, Carlow*, pp 40-48 has Agha also known as Achadh Finglaiss. Nearby lived the lords of Idrone; O'Curry, *Manners and customs*, ii, 68. I assume Cell Osna(i)d(h)' was so called at the date of the battle; Ryan, *Carlow*, p.21; Smyth, *Celtic Leinster*, p.32, plate xii.

4. O'Hanlon, *Lives*, iv, p.211.

5. U.C.D. Folklore MS 907, pp 34-5. The Department of Folklore asked me to abbreviate the proprietor's name.

6. O'Hanlon, *Lives*, iv, 211-2; MacNeill, *Lughnasa*, p.689 at 'stone chair'; 'St Laserian's well, Lorum' in O'Toole, 'Holy wells of Co. Carlow', pp 16-17; *Arch. inv. Carlow*, pp 58, 76. There were at least two earlier churches at Lorum before the present one was built. A well at Lorum has also been recorded as 'Molappog's Well'. The opening of a spring may have (been) relocated, giving rise to confusion as to whether there was one 'well' or two. Sketched at Lorum in 1890 was the base of an old stone cross. The dimensions of its base were given as '2 feet six inches long by 1 foot 6 inches broad, and 18 inches over ground'. This is clearly different from that object which was given as 'a strange column of granite', being 'perfectly circular', three and a half feet in diameter and two feet high and having a round hole in a flat topped centre. This was probably a 'culm crusher', pulled around by an ass and used in Carlow and Kilkenny to crush coal mixed with certain clay in order to make stick-shaped 'boms' or 'bums' for domestic fires. This latter object was said in 1989 to have been 'buried by local yobbos in a nearby bog some years ago'. Teampall Molaise in Ballinree townland is relatively modern and St Lazerian's at Kildavin was built 1827-42 (*Assoc. Pres. Mem. Dead, Irl.*, i, no.2 (1889), pp 68-9; O.P.W. topographical file, Carlow, 19:11; *O.S. letters, Carlow*; MacSuibhne, *Cluain na nGall*, p.19).

7. *Newsletter* (Leighlin parish, 1975), p.18; Bewley, 'Notes on a gallaun or pillar stone at Leighlin', pp 64-6. The stone is approximately 7 ft. high, is quite flat on the side facing Mount Leinster and has cup marks on the side towards Slieve Margy. It is a few hundred yards up the Nurney road from Leighlinbridge.

8. Illustration and report from *Anthologica Hibernica*, Oct. 1793, pp 274-5; Waddell, 'Irish bronze age cists', p.109.

9. *Metrical Dindshenchas,* iii, 3-25; MacNeill, *Lughnasa,* pp 339-44, 675; Byrne, *Celts,* p.163; Smyth, *Celtic Leinster,* pp 33-5, 117 and plate xii; In the context of athletic competitions at the fair is it significant that 'Fraochan the quarrelsome' challenged Oscar, son of Oisín, to single combat 'in Leithgleann' (*Duanaire Finn, pt. 1,* p.162)? Oscar has a 'grave' on Arran.

10. *Metrical Dindshenchas,* iii, 3-25; U.C.D. Folklore MS 907, pp 2, 26; *Leighlin Parish magazine* (1975), p.17.

11. O'Hanlon, *Lives,* iv, 214-5. While the name of the stream may conjure up the healing properties of Roman spas, it is taken locally to derive from an Irish word signifying heavy, wet land (Doyle, *Lazerian's Leighlin,* p.32). Fr John Aughney tells me that he has also seen the stream referred to in a document as the 'Divallagh'. U.C.D. Folklore MS 907, p.4, suggests that the name 'Cumar' was applied to the valley through which this stream runs but locals told the author that 'cumar' is used for any ditch or drain. Is it conceivable that this Raheen was that 'Ardarema' ('Ard': high) which Cormac granted to Comghall?

12. *Leighlin Parish magazine,* p.18; U.C.D. Folklore MS 907, p.3 for 'Cruckeen' in To[w]nasock ('tamhnac soc': sedgy, spewy land).

13. O'Hanlon, *Lives,* iv, 212-3; Baring-Gould and Fisher, *Lives,* iii, pp 42, 143-7 for a St Govan of Wales; *Encyclopaedia of Irish folk tradition,* pp 241-47, 276; Ryan, *Carlow,* p.21. There are seven persons in the Irish calendars bearing in some form the name Gob[b]án. The one geographically closest to Gobanus of Leighlin is Goban Mairge of Tascoffin. Tascoffin is in the barony of Gowran in County Kilkenny, in the Johnswell Mountains, which are a continuation of the Slieve Mairge. There is little known about this saint whose feast-day was 23 May. The 23 May was also the feast of one St Straphanus or Stephen, who had two brothers who were saints, one of whom was also called Gobbanus and one Lasrenus. The brothers were among the twelve disciples of St Mochuda, patron of Lismore in Munster. The latter Gobbanus was considered to be a bishop and shares a feast-day with Ireland's national saint, on 17 March. His brother Lasrenus (also Laseranus) was remembered on 25 October and is not considered to be identical with Laisren of Leighlin, although he happens to have been venerated at Ard mac Nasca on Belfast Lough, not far from our subject's place of birth and to have been of the Nasci. For his part brother Straphanus or Stephen was associated with Cluan Mór, believed to be Clonmore in the barony of Rathvilly, Co. Carlow. It may be noted that there was in Leighlin a priory of St Stephen, although a suggestion that it was named in honour of this obscure saint rather than the more famous martyr, Stephen, is unconvincing. (*Acta S.S.,* p.631; O'Hanlon, *Lives* 17 March, 23 May, 25 Oct.).

14. U.C.D. Folklore MS 907, pp 34-5.

15. *Arch. inv. Carlow*, pp 40, 48; Smyth, *Celtic Leinster*, p.38 indicates that the founders of monastic settlements usually avoided both high ground and the ill-drained boggy flats.

16. O'Hanlon, *Lives*, iv, p. 212; U.C.D. Folklore MS 907, p.41 appears to tell this particular tale of Gobbán himself.

17. Chadwick, *Saints in the early Celtic church*, p.133 n2; Brooke, *Wild men and holy places, passim*; *Arch. inv. Carlow*, pp 13, 35.

18. U.C.D. Folklore, MS 907, p.43.

19. *Cal. Oengus*, p. cclxxxiv gives per *Place-names of Ireland*, p.416: Lethglenn, now Leighlin. gen. sg. Lethglinde, leithglinne.

20. Dineen, p.646.

21. *Rennes Dindshenchas*, xv, 445 and xvi, 164; *A.F.M.* at 2,535 (p.7), at 1580AD (p.1,731); Hogan, *Onomasticon*, pp 503, 630.

6: Abbot Laisren of Leighlin

1. Nelson and Walsh, *Trees of Ireland*, p.71 for traditions of the hazel.

2. Plummer, *Vitae SS Hib.*, s.v. Molua, p.217 for the original Latin, translated above for the author by Fr James Smyth S.J.

3. Carney, *Irish literature and history,* p.263.

4. Bannerman, *History of Dalriada*, p.87; Anderson, *Kings and kingship in early Scotland*, p.149. Aedán is reportedly buried at Kilkerran in Kintyre.

5. *Adomnán's Life of Columba*, p.25.

6. ibid., Kenney, *Sources*, pp 210-21; O Cróinín, *Early medieval Ireland*, pp 152-4.

7. Heist, *Vitae Sanctorum*, p.343n. It is said that Kieran and others erected an abbey near Carlow about 634 (Ryan, *Carlow*, pp 21-2). The Fitzsimon version (S.7) omits any mention of Kieran having asked Laisren to go to Rome, saying instead that he had set out this time for the holy city 'at the request of Columba and of the kings and the saints already mentioned'. However, Colum Cille had died in 597 and one of the 'kings', Aedán, had died in 608. The Salamanca manuscript mentions Colum Cille's influence in connection with Laisren's earlier visit to Rome. The Arthur manuscript omits any mention of other saints or kings in this context, stating simply that this time Saint Laisren went to the apostolic site with fifty holy men.

8. *Irish litanies*, pp 120-21; Mann, *Lives of the popes*, pp 324-6.

9. Arthur gives this holy man as 'Mochomot'. Perhaps he was St Mochoemog, who died in old age in 656 and who was associated with Munster. He has

dedications in Scotland, where he came to be regarded as a female saint, Kevoca (Plummer, *Vitae SS Hib.*, p. lxxv, lxxviii).

10. Plummer, *Vitae SS Hib.*, s.v. Munnu, pp 236-7; *Acta S.S.* at 10 Jan. (St Tomian), n.8 gives '*synodus Lenensis sive Lethglennensis*' (see also for this *O.S. letters, Carlow*, pp 54-5).

11. Eusebius, *Ecclesiastical History*; Walsh, Cummian's Pascal letter, pp 147-8.

12. Plummer, *Vitae SS Hib.*, s.v. Munnu, pp 236-7. Slievemargy is the barony immediately west of the barony of Idrone West, wherein lies Leighlin.

13. 'On the feast of St Laeserian', at Comerford, *Leighlin*, i, 44-5, translated by Fr James Smyth S.J. for the author. For the dispute over Easter see also Hughes, *The church in early Irish society*, pp 103-10.

14. Kenney, *Sources*, pp 210-21; Hogan, *Onomasticon*, pp 511-2. One author suggests that Leighlin 'was originally called *Leighthlannia*, which supposedly corresponds in meaning with the English name *White Plain*', but he fails to advance any rationale for that supposed and unlikely correspondence (Comerford, *Kildare and Leighlin*, iii, 1 citing Dr John Lynch). Ailbe was the name of a queen of the Uí Garrchon of Leinster. Kenney says too that 'Ailbe was the name of the divine hound of Mac Dá-thEo, from which the great plain of Mag n-Ailbe was said to take its name'. In the very early Christian period in Ireland there was also a saint called Ailbe, who was known as 'the Patrick of Munster' (*Metrical Dindshenchas*, v, 149; *Thes. Pal.*, ii, 297n; Kenney, *Sources*, pp 221 nn 184, 314, no. 122 for 'Life of St Ailbe'; *Martyrology of Oengus*, pp 207 (12 Sept.) and 390 for Mag n-Ailbe, which is sometimes equated with Moynalvy, Kilmore, Co. Meath, but more usually placed in Co. Carlow and Co. Kilkenny).

15. *State Papers, Henry VIII*, vol. II, pt. 3 (1834), p.501; *Cal.S.P.Ire. (1509-73)*, p.37.

16. *Reg. of Deeds*, no. 37/66/21408.

17. Above, ch. 5, n.17; *Martyrology of Oengus*, p.248 gives a Banbán, as bishop of Lethglenn (26 Nov.).

18. U.C.D. Folklore MS 907, pp 36, 43, 165-6.

7: The strange death of 'a noble deacon'

1. *LL (Book of Leinster)*, cols 285b-286a. For which see Pokorny, 'Eine altirische legende', pp 207-15; Pokorny, 'Altirische texte', pp 235-41; *Book of Lismore*, p. x. Although published in German over eighty years ago, there has until now been no English translation of these passages or of most of the Book of Leinster. I am grateful to Dr Bríona Nic Dhiarmada of U. C. D. for the present translation. By coincidence, Dr Máirín Ní Dhonnchadha has simultaneously

translated the story for inclusion in the supplementary volume of the Field Day anthology of Irish writing.

2. Bergin, 'A mystical interpretation of the *Beati*', pp 103-06, The Book of Psalms, containing 150 psalms or 'the three fifties', was learnt off by heart by many Irish monks and played a central role in the 'Culdee' reform movement (O'Dwyer, *Céli Dé, passim*).

3. Ch. 1, n. 5, above; 'Account of Maignenn' (British Library MS); 'Betha Maignenn' (Bibliothèque Nationale Paris MS); Kenny, *Kilmainham*, pp 16-17. The author has placed facsimile copies of the two Maignenn manuscripts, which are similar, in the Royal Irish Academy, Dublin.

4. *Cal. Oengus*, p.lxxv.

5. Stokes, 'St Moling', pp 258, 281, 289; O'Curry, *Manners and Customs*, ii, 330; iii, 34; *Arch. inv. Carlow* for remains at St. Mullins.

6. LL (*Book of Leinster*), col. 200a, 12; Stokes, *Edinburgh Dindshenchas*, p.678; *Cal. Oengus*, pp clxxxi-ii which gives the Mugna as a yew.

7. *Martyrology of Oengus*, pp 193, 207, 387; Hogan, *Onomasticon*, 312,

8. *Book of Arran*, ii, 291-4, 303.

9. Carney, *Studies in Irish literature and history*, p.262; Kenney, *Sources*, p.216; O'Curry, *MS materials*, pp 404-6, 423-30; *Cal. Oengus*, p. cxliv.

10. *Cal. Oengus*, p.lxix; *Cronicum Scotorum*, pp 86-7.

11. See note 3 above.

12. *N. S. A.*, v, 6 states that instances of longevity on Arran 'are numerous'.

13. Pennant, *Scotland*, p.184, who gives the saint as 'Maol-jos' but, nevertheless, identifies him as the same saint who lived on Holy Island. For more on this name see the appendix; *Orig. Paroch.*, pp 254, 256; Headrick, *Arran*, pp 154, 167, 175; *Gazetteer of Scotland*, at 'Arran'.

14. *N.S.A.*, v, 54. The author adds, 'The ruins of an oratory or cell belonging to a monk called John, and containing the remains of the saint, stand on the farm of Balnacula'. Balnacoole farmhouse is half a mile from Clauchan.

15. *Arch. Journal*, iii, 136; McArthur, *Antiquities of Arran*, pp 170-2.

16. Ware, 'Bishops', pp 40-41; *Book of Clanranald*, pp 156-7; *Cal. papal reg.*, i, 8. Gwynn and Hadcock, *Med. religious houses*, p.89; *Synod of Argyll*, i, 65n; *Book of Arran*, i, 234, 240. A modern ferry service between Antrim and Kintyre has recently commenced summer sailings.

17. *Book of Arran*, i, 240.

18. Ibid.; McArthur, *Antiquities of Arran*, pp 170-2; 'On the feast of St Laeserian', at Comerford, *Leighlin*, i, 44-5.

19. Hall, *Tramping in Arran*, pp 24-6; Walton, *Walks in Arran*, pp 56-7. The median line of 'The Pilgrims' Way' approximates northing 31 on OS sheet 69.

20. *Book of Arran*, ii, 85-6; *Place-names of Arran*, p.88; Cameron, *Church in Arran*, pp 59-61. See also ch. 3, note 21, above for the cross. Across Clauchan Glen from Cnoc na Croise are 'Cnoc a Chapuill' ('Hill of the horse', unless 'Chapuill' is a late Anglicisation and a chapel stood here) and 'Cnoc na Dáil' ('hill of meetings'), which suggests a focus point for the people of the island. This name is perhaps a reference to Gaelic or Viking assemblies. Near these hills a path from Corriecravie and Sliddery, up by Grenree, met 'The Pilgrims' Way' and was used by migrant workers into the twentieth century. A local man told me that these would leave after midnight, meeting others en route from Shiskine and Blackwaterfoot and together making an early ferry for work in Glasgow. During World War II commandoes trained by crossing at night from Lamlash to Shiskine, according to one local farmer who recalls them being in his kitchen.

8: Wells

1. Roberston, 'Tour', p.18.

2. Pennant, *Scotland*, p.188; Headrick, *Arran*, pp 80-81.

3. Milne, *Arran*, p.21; Ruddock (née Kelso), 'Those were the days'.

4. Colin Cowley to the author, 31 Oct. 1996; Glasgow University Archaeological Research Division (GUARD) was invited to become involved in an advisory capacity in the Holy Island project. In June 1994 GUARD conducted a preliminary survey of aspects of the island's heritage. I am grateful to Ms Rachel Harry of GUARD for allowing me to read her unpublished typescript report.

5. U.C.D. Folklore MS 907, p.43.

6. O'Hanlon, *Lives*, iv, 214.

7. O'Toole, 'Holy wells of Carlow', p.15.

8. U.C.D. Folklore MS 907, p.211.

9. Letter from Wm Domville, 6 Jan. 1782 (T.C.D. MS 883/2, formerly I. i. 3, p.322).

10. U.C.D. Folklore Dept. MS 907, p.110.

11. Neary, 'Pilgrimages', *passim*; Kenny, *Kilmainham*, pp 46-7, 54, 71-2. 86-87.

12. Seward, *Topographia Hibernica*; O.S. letters, Carlow, p.65 f.

13. Lucas, 'Sacred trees', p.40; Milner, *Tree book*, p.138.

14. *O.S. letters, Carlow*, p.66; *Parliamentary gazetteer*, p.601; O'Hanlon, *Lives*, iv, 214-5. For a grainy photograph of the cross at its old location at the end of the nineteenth century see *Carloviana* n.s., xliv (1996), p.15.

15. O'Toole, 'Holy wells of Carlow', p.15; Mould, *Irish saints*, p.204.

16. O'Toole, 'Holy wells of Carlow', p.15.

17. U.C.D. Folklore MS 907, pp 43, 210.

18. ibid., pp 26, 31, 43; Minute books of meetings of the committee for repair of Saint Lazerian's well (MSS in the possession of Ms Mary MacDonald of Leighlinbridge, daughter of a committee member, Ed MacDonald, who believed that his family was of Scottish origin).

19. U.C.D. Folklore MS 907, p.210.

20. *The* [Carlow] *Nationalist*, 29 April 1994; *Wicklow Times*, 14 Feb. 1996; *Old Leighlin Foróige Journal*, ii (Spring, 1996).

21. Lawton, *Aifreann Laserian*, introduction.

9: Remembering Molaise

1. *Irish litanies*, p.75. These Ernans or Erníns were both celebrated as saints. It seems that one of them may have been the son of a brother of Laisren, who was called Finan or Findchán.

2. *A.F.M.* at 690.

3. *Irish litanies*, p.75.

4. Doyle, *Lazerian's Leighlin*, p.11. The existence of a later Augustinian leper hospital may have given rise to this memory.

5. *A.F.M.* at 1113; Archdall, *Mon. Hib.*, pp xvii-iii ; For 'coarbs' and 'erenaghs' see Nicholls, *Gaelic and Gaelicised Ireland*, pp 111-13.

6. *Book of Clanranald*, pp 156-7; Robertson, 'Tour', p.18; *Book of Arran*, i, 224, 257-60. Was this that 'cottage near the shore' to which reference has been made at ch. 3, note 22, above?

7. Dowling, *Annals*, pp ii, xx; Ware, 'Bishops', p.44 and 'Writers', p.26; Comerford, *Kildare and Leighlin*, i, 56. According to Ware, *Works concerning Ireland*, i, 456, as edited by Harris, a later bishop of Leighlin and Ferns 'left behind him a library for the use of his clergy, which was afterwards utterly destroyed in the Rebellion of 1641'. This may explain the loss of the Book of Leighlin and other records.

8. Nat. Museum, R. 3057; Armstrong, *Irish seals*, p.70; History of the cathedral church of St Laserian, AD 651-1869 (R.C.B. Library MS), p.37, adds that, subsequent to its discovery, the matrix was purchased by Rev. S. Madden, who gave it to Dean Dawson. This may be the matrix of that seal of the chapter to which reference is found in 1310. A bishop's seal was also mentioned that year. Portion of a seal, showing a bishop with his crozier, appears on a deed of absolution and dispensation for schism and irregularity granted by Thomas, bishop of Leighlin, in 1558. The current cathedral matrix appears to date from 1699 and has not the same motif as the above (Ware, 'Bishops', p.41; *Cal. just. rolls, Ire., 1308-14*, p.165 (1310); *Ir. mon. deeds, 1200-1600*, pp 199-201).

9. *Festa propria quorundam Hib. SS.*, cited at Comerford, *Leighlin*, i, 44-45 and iii, 408-9. Translated for the author by Fr James Smyth S.J. St Paul wrote, 'I have become all things to all men, that I might by all means save some' (1 *Cor.* 9:22). More than one later follower of Jesus has been posthumously helped towards this same strategy by historical revisionism.

10. Cowley MS: Huston to Laidlaw, 29 June 1960; Arran Estate Office, Holy Island correspondence files, 1958-9, esp. A. MacMillan, district clerk, Bute Co. Council, Arran local committee, to Messrs J. C. & A. Stewart, 28 Jan. 1959; ibid., 12 Nov. 1965.

11. Ibid. A bound copy of McCallum's typed report (2 vols) is in the Isle of Arran Museum (MS 277).

12. Telephone interview, Kay Morris with the author; Thompson, 'The dream that came true', which also noted Kay's hope that her sister, an archaeologist in Dublin, might have the opportunity to examine the island. She never did; *Ev. Times*, 19 Sept. 1985; *The Times,* 12 Nov. 1991; *Sunday Mail*, 12 Nov. 1989. I am grateful to the Universities Federation for Animal Welfare for sending me extracts from their annual reports and a leaflet. Some of the larger animals left on the island by UFAW later got into difficulty and attracted adverse publicity before being evacuated ('Horror in Holy Isle' and 'Island of death' in *Sunday Mail*, 12 Nov. 1989).

13. Carter, 'Where east meets west', pp 27-30; McCarthy, 'Holy Island', p.4.

14. Ibid.

15. *Arran Banner*, 2 Nov. 1991, 2 and 23 Nov. 1991 and 23 May 1992; *The Times*, 12 Nov. 1991; *The Guardian*, 23 Nov. 1991; *The Scotsman*, 23 Nov. 1991; Mailshot appeal from Lama Yeshe, 8 Dec. 1991; Michael, bishop of St Andrews, to Samye Ling, 25 May 1992 (Holy Island boxes, Samye Ling). The late Dom Houédard ('dsh') was renowned for his work with non-Christians and some of his photocopies in the Holy Island boxes at Samye Ling proved useful to this

author. He died on 15 Jan. 1992 at the age of 67. Four years earlier Houédard and the bishop had taken part in a symposium at Samye Ling. He attended the opening of the temple there, soliciting and conveying a special message of congratulations and very best wishes from Cardinal Francis Arinze, president of the Vatican's Pontifical Council for Interreligious Dialogue. (Whaling and Holmes, *The Samye symposia, no.1, passim*; *The Guardian*, 29 Jan. 1992; Secretary, Prinknash Abbey, to the author, 18 April 1996; dsh archive (The John Rylands Research Institute MSS, *passim*, incl. boxes 59, 67)).

16. *Arran Banner*, 25 April 1992.

17. Ibid. Mr Adamson also informs the author that the Buddhists are 'very approachable, nice kind of people' and denies a rumour that the Free Masons were opposed to their acquisition of the island. He writes that, 'Freemasonry also promotes the universal brotherhood of man. We do not allow religious or political discussion at our meetings and so have categorically *no* objection to the Buddhists on Holy Island'. He notes that they chose the name St Molios for their lodge, 'simply because many, many lodges chose the name of a local saint' (Letter to the author, 10 Feb. 1997).

18. *The Scotsman*, 8 June 1972; *Arran Banner*, 30 Nov. 1991, 25 April 1992 and 23 May 1992; *News of the World*, 18 Jan. 1992 ('Buddha off! Monks ban locals from Holy Island'); *The Times*, Saturday Review cover-story, 8 Feb. 1992 ('A Buddhist brings new faith to Holy Island'); *The Holy Island Project Newsletter 1993*, p.5; Macgregor, *Scotland*, p.103.

19. 'Lama Yeshe interview', in *Holy Island Project Newsletter, 1993*, p.19,

20. 'First steps to success: planning permission granted', in *Holy Island Project News, 1996*, pp 8-9; The web-site of the Holy Island Project, (http://www.samye.org/isle.html), Jan. 1997. Amongst the many crews visiting Holy Island was one making a documentary for RTE. This was screened during 1997 ('Communities of Faith: the Samye Ling community').

21. See also Lowe, 'Holy Island architectural competition', pp 7-8; Finch, Jennings and Battle, 'Combining technology and nature on Holy Island', pp 32-8.

22. See n.20 above for web-site.

23. Merton, *Asian Journal, passim*. The present author first visited Samye Ling, Scotland, in Jan. 1976.

Appendix

1. *Calendar of Oengus*, pp lxxv, cxxx, cxlv, lxix; *LL (Book of Leinster)*, cols 349d, 372b; Smyth, *Celtic Leinster*, p.102.

2. *Cal. Oengus*, lvii, cclxxxii.

3. *Book of Clanranald*, pp 156-7; Monro, *Western isles*, p.486; Buchanan, *History of Scotland*, p.24; Bremner, *Norsemen in Alban*, pp 250-51; Anderson, *Sources*, ii, 608-42.

4. In 1840 the minister of Kilbride, the easternmost of Arran's two parishes, wrote that 'among the rural population, Gaelic is decidedly the prevailing language'. His colleague in the west added that the language 'universally spoken' by his parishioners was Gaelic. By 1915 it had 'ceased to be the language of the playground and is therefore doomed to speedy extinction'. By 1931, it was said, the total number of Gaelic speakers was just 605 out of a population of 4, 532 people on Arran. But in 1938 Holmer could find not a single individual who used it in everyday speech. One of the last Gaelic speakers is said to have been Mrs Kelso of Holy Island. In the end it took barely a century to sweep away the old language (*N.S.A.*, v., 26, 54; *S.H.R.*, xii (1915), p.419; Holmer, *Gaelic of Arran, passim*; McLellan, *Isle of Arran*, pp 29, 63; Milne, *Arran*, ch. 9: 'The tongue of Eden'; O Baóill, Ulster Irish and Scottish Gaelic, pp 9-28: 'Ireland and Arran'; Barrow, *Scotland*, pp 104-26: 'The lost Gaidhealtachd'). Campbell noted that where at least 50% of Scots spoke Gaelic as their principal language in the sixteenth century, only 20% spoke it by 1801, 10% by 1861 and 2% by 1931(Campbell, *Gaelic in Scottish education and life*, p. 33). *Book of Arran*, ii, 367 and 314-50 for a collection of Gaelic songs of Arran.

5. *Cronicum Scotorum*, pp 86-7; *Arran place-names*, p.6.

6. Pennant, *Scotland*, pp 184, 188. Camden, *Britannia*, ed. Gough, p.338 for confirmation that in 1789 they were regarded as the same; *Orig. Paroch.*; Cameron, *Church in Arran*, pp 31-2; *Book of Arran*, i, 240; ibid., ii, 69, n.1.

7. Cameron, *Church in Arran*, p.31.

8. *Book of Arran*, ii, 76-7; Fordun, i. 13 and ii, 39 gives 'Bladay' for Pladda.

9. Headrick, *Arran*, p.80; Holmer, *Gaelic of Arran*, pp 6, 45.

10. Copy letter, encl. copy of McLellan's memo, from A. MacMillan, district clerk, to Messrs J. C.& A. Stewart, Edinburgh, 28 Jan. 1959 (Arran Estate Office, Holy Isle correspondence files).

11. *Book of Leinster*, vi, 1543; *Adomnán's Life of Columba*, p. xxxviii and paras 5a, 5b, 20b, 23b-24a., 31a-b; *Martyrology of Oengus* and *Martyrology of Tallaght, passim* for feast-days; *A.F.M.*, at 601; *Cronicum Scotorum*, pp 69, 86-7; *Book of Lismore*, pp 191-2, 300, 328, 336; O'Hanlon, *Lives*, i, 79; Gwynn, 'St Lasair', pp 73-103; MacNeill, *Lughnasa,* pp 168-9; Smyth, *Celtic Leinster*, p.82.

Bibliography

MANUSCRIPTS

Arran Estate Office
Holy Island correspondence files, twentieth-century.
Feu disposition by the commissioners for the trustees of the late duke of Hamilton
in favour of the Commissioners of Northern Lighthouses, 1903.

Bibliothèque Nationale Paris
Betha Maignenn (Fonds Celtique et Basque, MS 1, ff 30-32).

Bibliothèque Royale, Brussels
Vita S. Lasriani seu Molaisse, abbatis de Lethglenn (MS 7672-41), printed in
W. Heist (ed.), *Vitae Sanctorum Hiberniae* (Brussels, 1965), pp.340-3.

British Library
Account of Maignenn (Egerton MS 91, new f.49).

Colin Cowley, private papers, Liverpool
Carbon copy of letter from Stewart Huston, owner of Holy Island, to George
Laidlaw, editor of the *Third Statistical Account of Scotland*, 29 June 1960.

Glasgow University Archaeological Research Division (GUARD)
Partial survey of Holy Island by Ms Rachel Harry (typescript).

Historic Scotland
Arran file notes.

Isle of Arran Museum
Letter: Margaret Fagg, née Paterson, to Isle of Arran Museum, 1983.

Leighlinbridge
Minute books of meetings of the committee for repair of Saint Lazerian's well
(MSS in the possession of Ms Mary MacDonald of Leighlinbridge).

Leighlin Cathedral
Record books, nineteenth and twentieth centuries.

National Library of Ireland
R. D. Walshe press cuttings, Carlow (N.L.I. MS 14,001).

Office of Public Works
Co. Carlow site files.

Co. Carlow: urban archaeological survey, by John Bradley and Heather A. King, n. d. (Typescript).

Representative Church Body Library, Dublin
Biographical succession list of the clergy of Leighlin diocese, by Canon B. Leslie, 1939, with some later insertions (2 vols).
History of the cathedral church of St Laserian, AD 651-1869.
Dean and chapter of the cathedral of St Laserian (alias Lazerian), Leighlin, Chapter Act Book 1719-1873.

Saint Patrick's College, Maynooth
A collection of lives of Irish saints, in Latin (MS 3 G 1 (RB 201)).

Samye Ling Centre, Eskdalemuir
Holy Island boxes (Press-cuttings, letters, photocopies, etc.).
Typescript translation into French of Fitzsimon's manuscript, from *Acta S.S.*, by François Chenique, made on 18 April 1991.

. *University College Dublin*
Department of Irish Folklore: Schools Manuscript 907 (AD 1938).
Maura Walsh, Cummian's Pascal letter (M. Phil., 1977).

Universities Federation for Animal Welfare, Herts.
Annual reports.

REFERENCE WORKS AND SOURCE COMPILATIONS

Account roll of the priory of the Holy Trinity Dublin. Ed. James Mills. Dublin, 1891.
Acts of the the lords of the isles, 1336-1493. Scot. Hist. Soc., 4s. xxii. Edinburgh, 1986.
A.F.M. (Annala ríoghacta Éireann; Annals of the kingdom of Ireland by the Four Masters from the earliest period to the year 1616. Ed. and trans. John O'Donovan. 7 vols. Dublin, 1851. Repr. New York, 1966).
'Agallamh na senórach' (Cited and translated from the Book of Lismore at *Silva Gadelica,* i, 102 & ii, viii, x-xi, 109).
Anderson, 'Lists of kings' (Anderson, M. O. The lists of the kings. In *Scottish Hist. Rev.*, xxix (1950)).
Anderson, *Sources* (Anderson, A. O. *Early sources of Scottish history 500-1286 AD.* Stamford, 1990).
Annals of Arran (Cowley, Colin. *Ye* [The] *Annals of Arran.* Limited circulation typescript, Lamlash, 1992).
Annals of Arran (Cowley, Colin. *Annals of Arran.* Revised. Limited circulation typescript, [Liverpool], 1996).
Archdall, *Mon. Hib.* (Mervyn Archdall. *Monasticon Hibernicum.* London, 1786).
Arch inv. Carlow (A. Brindley and A. Kilfeather (eds). *Archaeological inventory of County Carlow.* Office of Public Works, Dublin, 1993).

Armstrong, *Seals* (Armstrong, E.C.R. *Irish seal matrices and seals*. Dublin 1913).

Arran book file. Ed. Colin Cowley. Limited circulation typescript, Lamlash, 1991. Rev. 1996.

Arran place-names (Alexander Cameron, *Arran place-names*. [Inverness], 1890).

Book of Arran (Vol. i. Ed. Balfour, J. A. Glasgow, 1910; Vol. ii. Ed. Mackenzie, W. M. Glasgow, 1914. Both repr. Brodick, 1982). For a review of *Book of Arran, ii*, see *S.H.R.*, xii (1915), pp 418-9.

Book of Clanranald (The Book of Clanranald. In *Reliquiae Celticae: texts, papers and studies in Gaelic literature and philosophy left by Alexander MacBain*. Ed A. MacBain and J. Kennedy. 2 vols. Inverness, 1884).

LL (Book of Leinster). (*The book of Leinster, sometime called the book of Glendalough*. Ed. Robert Atkinson. Dublin, 1880).

Book of Leinster. Ed. O'Sullivan, Best et al. Dublin, 1954-83.

Book of Lismore. Ed. Whitley Stokes. Oxford, 1890.

Carmina Gadelica (*Carmina Gadelica: hymns and incantations collected in the highlands and islands of Scotland and translated into English*. By Alexander Carmichael. Edinburgh, 6 vols. 1900-1940).

Celtic place-names (Watson, William (ed.). *The history of the Celtic place-names of Scotland*. Edinburgh, 1926).

Comerford, *Kildare and Leighlin* (Comerford, A.M. *Collections relating to the dioceses of Kildare and Leighlin*. 3 vols, Dublin, [1886]).

Concise Scots English dictionary. Ed. Mairi Robinson. Aberdeen, 1985.

Cowan and Easson, *Med. religious houses* (Cowan, I.B. and Easson, D.E. *Medieval religious houses in Scotland*. 2nd ed., London and New York, 1976).

Cronicum Scotorum (*Cronicum Scotorum*. Ed. Wm Hennessy. London, 1866).

Dowling, *Annals* (Butler, Richard (ed.). *The annals of Ireland by Friar John Clyn and Thady Dowling*. Dublin, 1849).

Dict. Ir. lang. Ed. Royal Irish Academy. Dublin, 1913-75.

Dineen (Dineen, Patrick. *Foclóir Gaedhilge agus Béarla*. Dublin, 1927).

Eusebius, *Ecclesiastical History* (Translated at Bindley, T.H. *Epistle of the Gallican Churches*. London, 1900).

Extents Ir. mon. possessions (*Extents of Irish monastic possessions, 1540-1541, from manuscripts in the Public Record Office, London*. Ed. Newport B. White. Dublin, 1943).

Facs. nat. MSS Ire. (*Facsimiles of the national manuscripts of Ireland*. Ed. J. T. Gilbert. 4 vols. Dublin, 1874-84).

Fasti Ecclesiae Scoticanae. Ed. Hew Scott. 8 vols, Edinburgh, 1915-50.

Fordun (de Fordun, Johannis. *Chronica Gentes Scotorum*. Ed. William Skene. 2 vols. Edinburgh, 1871).

Gaelic Dict. (Edward Dwelly (ed.). *Illustrated Gaelic Dictionary*. 3 vols. Herne Bay, 1901-11).

Gazetteer of the British Isles (Bartholomew, John (ed.). 9th. ed., Edinburgh, 1943).

Gazetteer of Scotland (Topographical, Statistical and Historical Gazetteer of Scotland. 2 vols. Glasgow, 1842).

Gwynn and Hadcock, *Med. religious houses* (Gwynn, Aubrey and Hadcock, R. N. *Medieval religious houses in Ireland.* London, 1970).

Harbison, *High crosses* (Harbison, Peter. *The high crosses of Ireland: an iconographical and photographic survey.* 3 vols. Bonn, 1992).

Hogan, *Onomasticon* (Hogan, Edmund. *Onomasticon Goedelicum locorum et tribuum Hiberniae et Scotiae.* Dublin, 1910).

Irish litanies (*Irish litanies.* Ed. Charles Plummer. London, 1905).

Ir. mon. deeds (*Irish monastic and episcopal deeds, AD 1200-1600, transcribed from the originals preserved at Kilkenny Castle, with an appendix of documents of the sixteenth and seventeenth centuries relating to monastic property after the dissolution.* Ed. N. B. White, Dublin, 1936).

Kenney, *Sources* (Kenney, J. F. *The sources for the early history of Ireland: an introduction and guide, vol.i: ecclesiastical.* New York, 1929).

McNeill, Charles (ed.). Report on recent acquisitions in the Bodleian Library, Oxford. In *Anal. Hib.*, i (1930).

Metrical Dindshenchas (*The metrical Dindshenchas.* Ed. Edward Gwynn, R.I.A. Todd lecture series, x. Dublin, 1913).

Misc. Scot.(*Miscellanea Scotica: a collection of tracts relating to the history, antiquities, topography and literature of Scotland.* 4 vols, Glasgow, 1818-20).

O'Curry, *Manners and customs* (O'Curry, Eugene. *On the manners and customs of the ancient Irish.* 3 vols. London, 1873).

O'Curry, *MS materials* (O'Curry, Eugene. *Lectures on the manuscript materials of ancient Irish history.* Dublin, 1861).

O.E.D. (*Oxford English Dictionary*).

Encyclopaedia of Irish folk tradition (O hOgain, Daithi. *An encyclopaedia of the Irish folk tradition.* New York, 1991).

O.S. letters, Carlow (*Letters containing information relative to the antiquities of the counties of...collected during the progress of the ordnance survey in 1835 [etc.],* reproduced under the direction of Rev. Michael O'Flanagan from the originals in the Royal Irish Academy. Typescript, 42 vols in 35 bindings. Bray, 1926-8).

Parliamentary gazetteer (Dublin and London, 1844).

Place-names of Arran (Currie, Ronald. *The place-names of Arran.* Glasgow, 1908).

Place-names of Carlow (O'Toole, Edward. *Place-names of Carlow.* Carlow, n. d. [1930s])

Place-names of Ireland (P. W. Joyce (ed.). *The origin and history of Irish names of places.* Dublin, 1895-1913).

Place-names of Scotland. Ed. J. B. Johnston. London, 1934.

Registrum Magni Sigilli.

Rennes Dindshenchas ('The Rennes Dindshenchas'. Ed. Whitley Stokes. In *Revue Celtique*, xv [1895], xvi [1896]).

Seward, *Topographia Hibernica* (Seward, William. *Topographia Hibernica*. Dublin, 1795).

Sheehy, *Pontificia Hib.* (Sheedy, M. P. (ed.). *Pontificia Hibernica: medieval papal chancery documents concerning Ireland, 640-1261*. 2 vols. Dublin, 1962, 1965).

Silva Gadelica (O'Grady, Standish (ed.) *Silva Gadelica: a collection of tales in Irish edited from manuscripts and translated*. 2 vols. London, 1892).

Supernatural Arran (Cowley, Colin, *Supernatural Arran*. Limited circulation typescript, Lamlash, 1992).

Synod of Argyle (*Minutes of the Synod of Argyle, 1639-1651*. Ed. Duncan MacTavish. Scot. Hist. Soc., vols 37 & 38. Edinburgh, 1943-44).

Thes. Pal., (*Thesaurus Palaeohibernicus: a collection of Old-Irish glosses, scholia, prose and verse*. Ed. Whitley Stokes and John Strachan, J. 2 vols. Cambridge, 1901-3).

SAINTS' BIOGRAPHIES, HAGIOGRAPHIES, MARTYROLOGIES, ETC.

Acta S.S. (*Acta sanctorum quotquot....Johannes Bollandus...[etc.]*, Antwerp [etc.] 1643-).

Adomnán's Life of Columba. Edited and translated by A. O. Anderson and M. O. Anderson. Oxford, 1991.

Baring-Gould, S and Fisher, J. *Lives of the British saints*. London, 1911.

Baring-Gould, S. *Lives of the saints*. 16 vols., London, new and rev. 1914.

Brooke, Daphne. *Wild men and holy places: St Ninian, Whithorn and the medieval realm of Galloway*. Edinburgh, 1994.

Vita S. Columba, by Adamnan. Ed. J. T. Fowler. Oxford, 1894.

Cal. Oengus (*On the calendar of Oengus*. Ed. Whitley Stokes. Dublin, 1880).

Gwynn, Lucius. The life of St Lasair. In *Ériu*, v (1911).

Healy, J. *Ireland's ancient saints and scholars*. 2nd ed., Dublin, 1893.

Heffernan, Thomas J., *Sacred biography: saints and their biographers in the Middle Ages*. Oxford, 1995. On this see *The Innes Review*, xlvi, no. 2 (Autumn, 1995).

Heist, W (ed.). *Vitae Sanctorum Hiberniae*. Brussels, 1965

Hughes, Kathleen. The cult of St Finnian of Clonard from the eighth to the eleventh century. In *I.H.S.*, ix (1954-5).

Lawton, Liam. *Molaise: Aifreann Laserian Naofa* [sung-Mass, Carlow, 1996].

MacQueen, John. Myths and legends of the lowland Scottish saints. In *Scot. Studies*, xxiv (1980).

Martyrology of Gorman. Ed. Whitley Stokes. Henry Bradshaw Soc., ix, London, 1895.

Martyrology of Oengus ['Felire Oengusso']. Ed. Whitley Stokes. Henry Bradshaw Soc., xxix, London, 1905.

Martyrology of Tallaght from the book of Leinster and MS 5100-4 in The Royal Library, Brussels. Ed. R. Irvine and H. Jackson Lawlor. London, 1931.

Metcalfe, William. *Legends of the saints*. Scot. Text. Soc., 3 vols, Edinburgh and London, [1887]-1896.

Mould, Daphe Pouchin. *The Irish saints*. Dublin and London, 1964.

O'Hanlon, *Lives* (John O'Hanlon. *Lives of the saints with special festivals, compiled from calendars, martyrologies and various sources.* 11 vols. Dublin, 1875-[1896]).

O Riain, Padraig. *Corpus genealogiarum sanctorum Hiberniae.* Dublin, 1985.

Pinkerton, John (ed.). *Vitae antiquae sanctorum qui habitaverunt in ea parte Britanniae nunc vocata Scotia vel in ejus insulis.* London, 1789.

Plummer, *Vitae SS Hib.* (Charles Plummer (ed.). *Vitae sanctorum Hiberniae, partim hactenus ineditae...* 2 vols. Oxford, 1910).

Power, Sister Declan. Saint Mo-Ling Luachra. In *Carloviana: Jn. of the Old Carlow Society*, n.s., xliv (1996).

Reeves, William. *Life of Columba, written by Adamnan.* Dublin, 1857.

Scott, Archibald. St Maolrubha. In *S.H.R.*, v (1908).

Sharpe, Richard. *Medieval Irish saints' lives: an introduction to vitae sanctorum Hiberniae.* Oxford, 1991.

Smith, John. *The life of Saint Columba...commonly called Colum-Kille, the apostle of the highlands.* Edinburgh, 1798.

'The birth and life of St Moling'. Ed. Whitley Stokes. In *Revue Celtique*, xxvii (1906).

BOOKS AND ARTICLES

Alaya, Flavia. *William Sharp, 1855-1905.* Harvard, 1970.

Anderson, M. O. *Kings and kingship in early Scotland.* Edinburgh, 1973.

Anon. The see of Leighlin. In *Ir. Eccles. Rec.*, ii (1866). Comerford, *Kildare and Leighlin*, i, 44 suggests Cardinal Moran as the author of this.

Anon. The green island. In *S H. R.*, v (1908).

Anon. Stone of Scone. In *S.H.R.*, viii (1911).

Balfour, J. A. The ecclesiastical remains in the Holy Island, Arran. In *P.S.A.S.*, xliii (1908-9).

Balfour, J. A. *The Book of Arran, vol. i.* Glasgow, 1910. Brodick, 1982.

Bannerman, John. *Studies in the history of Dalriada.* Edinburgh, 1974.

Bannerman, John. The lordship of the isles. In Brown, *Scottish society*.

Barley, M. W. and Hanson, R. P. C. *Christianity in Britain, 300-700.* Leicester, 1968.

Barrow, G. W. S. *Kingship and unity: Scotland 1000-1306. N.H.S.*, ii, London, 1981.

Barrow, G. W. S. *Scotland and its neighbours in the middle ages.* London and Rio Grande, 1992. No. 6: The lost Gaidhealtachd.

Bateson, J.D. Roman and medieval coins found in Scotland, to 1987. In *P.S.A.S.*, cix (1989).

Bergin, Osborne and Marstrander, Carl (eds). *Miscellany presented to Kuno Meyer,* Halle, 1912.

Bergin, Osborn. A mystical interpretation of the *Beati.* In *Ériu*, xi (1932).

Bewley, Edmund. Notes on a gallaun or pilar stone at Leighlin, Co. Carlow. In *JRSAI*, xxxv (1905).

Bieler, Ludwig. The Christianisation of the insular Celts during the sub-Roman period and its repercussions on the continent. In *Celtica*, viii (1968).

Bowen, E. G. *Saints, seaways and settlements*. Cardiff, 1969.

Bremner, Robert. *The Norsemen in Alban*. Glasgow, 1923.

Brenneman, Mary and Walter. *Crossing the circle at the holy wells of Ireland*.
   University of Virginia, 1995.

Brown, A. L. The Cistercian Abbey of Saddell, Kintyre. In *Innes Review*, xx (1969).

Buchanan, George. *History of Scotland*. London, 1690.

Burleigh, J. H. S. *A church history of Scotland*. Oxford, 1960.

Byrne, F. J. *Irish kings and high-kings*. London, 1973.

Camden, William. *Britannia: or a geographical description of Great Britain and Ireland*.
   Ed. Richard Gough. 3 vols. London, 1789.

Cameron, J. K. *The church in Arran from the earliest period to the present day*.
   Edinburgh, 1912.

Campbell, Ewan. A cross-marked quern from Dunadd and other evidence for
   relations between Dunadd and Iona. In *P.S.A.S.*, cxvii (1987).

Campbell, John F. *Popular tales of the west highlands*. 4 vols. Edinburgh, 1862.

Campbell, John Lorne. *Gaelic in Scottish education and life: past, present and future*.
   Edinburgh, 1945.

Carney, James. *Studies in Irish literature and history*. Dublin, 1979.

Carey, John. Suibhne Geilt and Túan Mac Cairill. In *Éigse*, xx (1984).

Carter, Winifred. Where east meets west: a Buddhist temple in south-west
   Scotland. In *Univ. Edinburgh Jn.*, xxxv, no. 1 (June, 1991).

Chadwick, H. M. *Early Scotland*. Cambridge, 1949.

Chadwick, N. K. *The age of the saints in the early Celtic church*. Oxford, 1961.

Chadwick, N. K. *Celtic Britain*. London, 1963.

Charles-Edwards, T. M. The social background to Irish *peregrinatio*. In *Celtica*,
   xi (1976).

Coburn, Henry. *Circuit Journey*. Hawick, 1983.

Connolly, Hugh. *The Irish penitentials and the sacrament of penance today*. Dublin, 1995.

Conway, Agnes. *Henry VII's relations with Scotland and Ireland, 1485-1498*.
   Cambridge, 1932.

Curry, Eugene (ed.). *The battle of Magh Leana*. Dublin, 1855.

Davies, Elizabeth. A pilgrimage. In *Holy Island Project Newsletter*. 1993.

Delany, Ruth. *A celebration of 250 years of Ireland's inland waterways*. Belfast, 1986.

Dillon, Myles and Chadwick, N. K. *The Celtic realms*. London, 1967.

Dillon, Myles. The consecration of Irish kings. *Celtica*, x (1973).

Dillon, Myles. The Irish settlements in Wales. In *Celtica*, xii (1977).

Donaldson, Gordon. *Church and nation through sixteen centuries*. London, 1960.

Downie, R. A. *The islands of the Clyde*. Perth, 1982.

Doyle, Margaret. *Lazerian's Leighlin: history of the parish of Leighlinbridge, Carlow*.
   Carlow, [c.1971].

Duncan, Archibald. *Scotland: the making of a kingdom*. Edinburgh, 1975.

Fairhurst, Horace. *Exploring Arran's past*. Brodick, 2nd ed. 1982, 3rd 1988.

Fenton, A. and Palsson, H. (eds), *The northern and western isles in the Viking world: survival, continuity and change* (Edinburgh, 1984).

Fernie, Mary. *Around the island of Arran*. s. l., 1985.

Finch, P., Jennings, N. and Battle, G. Combining technology and nature on Holy Island. In *The Architects' Jn.*, 18 April 1996.

Firsoff, V. A. *Arran with camera and sketchbook*. London, 1951.

Flower, Robin. *The Irish Tradition*. Oxford, 1948 and 1966.

Frame, Robin. The Bruces in Ireland, 1315-18. In *I.H.S.*, xix (1974).

Friell, J. G. P. and Watson, W. G. (eds). *Pictish studies: settlement, burial and art in Dark Age northern Britain*. Oxford, BAR British series, cxxv (1984).

Gemmell, Alastair. *Discovering Arran*. Edinburgh, 1990.

Giblin, Cathaldus. *The Irish Franciscan mission to Scotland, 1619-1646: documents from Roman archives*. Dublin, 1964.

Giraldus, *The autobiography of Giraldus Cambrensis*. Ed. and translated by H. E. Butler. London, 1937.

Giraldus, *Expugnatio Hibernia: the conquest of Ireland by Giraldus Cambrensis*. Ed. A. B. Scott and F. X. Martin. Dublin, 1978.

Glasgow University Archaeological Research Division (GUARD). *Archaeological survey at the King's Caves, Arran*. Glasgow, 1994.

Green, Miranda. *Symbol and image in Celtic religious art*. London, 1989.

Grinsell, Leslie V., *Folklore of pre-historic sites in Britain*. Devon, 1976.

Gregory, Donald. *The history of the western highlands and islands of Scotland*. 1493-1625. Edinburgh, 1836. Repr. 1975.

Grose, Francis. *Antiquities of Scotland*. 2 vols. London, 1791.

Grose, Francis. *Antiquities of Ireland*. 2 vols. Dublin, 1792.

Gwynn, Aubrey. *The Irish church in the eleventh and twelfth centuries*. Dublin, 1992.

Hall, Charles. *Isle of Arran*. London, 1912.

Hall, Ken. *South Arran: a postcard tour*. Ayrshire, 1994.

Hall, T. S. *Tramping in Arran*. Falkirk, 3rd ed. rev. 1947.

Hayden, Margaret. The district of Leighlin: Laserian's country. In *Carloviana*, n. s., ii, (1981).

Hayes-McCoy, G. A. *Scots mercenary forces in Ireland, 1565-1603*. Dublin and London, 1937.

Headrick, James. *View of ...the island of Arran*. Edinburgh, 1807.

Holinshed, Raphael. *Chronicles of Great Britain and Ireland,* [Ed. John Hooker, 1586]. 6 vols. London, 1808.

Holmer, Nils. *The Gaelic of Arran*. Dublin, 1957.

Hudson, Benjamin T. *Kings of Celtic Scotland*. Westport, Connecticut, and London, 1994.

Hughes, John Scott. *Harbours of the Clyde*. London, 1954.

Hughes, Kathleen. *The church in early Irish society*. London, 1966.

Hume Brown, P. The moulding of the Scottish nation. In *S H.R.*, i (1904).

Jackson, Kenneth (ed.). *Cath Maighe Léne*. Dublin, 1938.

Jackson, K. H. The motive of the three-fold death in the story of Suibhne Geilt. In *Essays and studies presented to Professor Eóin MacNéill*. Dublin, 1940.

Keating, *Foras feasa* (Geoffrey Keating, *Foras feasa ar Éirinn; The history of Ireland*. Ed. D. Comyn and P. S. Dineen. 4 vols. London, 1902-14).

Kenny, Colum. *Kilmainham: the history of a settlement older than Dublin*. Dublin, 1995.

Kenny, Colum. Laserian's Scottish connection. In *Carloviana*, n. s., xliv (1996).

Kenny, Colum. New Leighlin: a forgotten Anglo-Norman settlement. Forthcoming.

Kerr-Hunter, J. A. Holy Isle. In *Scottish Field*, cvi, no. 679 (July 1959).

Kersley Holmes. Holy Island. Misidentified cutting, c.1959 (Samye Ling).

Knight, G. A. *Archaeological light on the early Christianising of Scotland*. 2 vols. London, 1933.

Knight, Barry. *St Molios, Shiskine, 1889-1989: a centenary guide*. Skiskine, 1989.

Laing, Lloyd and Laing, Jennifer. Scottish and Irish metalwork and the '*conspiratio barbarica*'. In *P.S.A.S.*, cxvi (1986)

Landsborough, David. *Excursions to Arran, Ailsa Craig and the two Cumbraes*. Edinburgh, 1852.

Landsborough, David. A sculptured cross, with cruciform on obverse, recently discovered at Lamlash. In *P.S.A.S.*, xxxi (1896-7).

Lane, Alan. Some Pictish problems at Dunadd. In Friell and Watson, *Pictish studies*,

Lanigan, John. *An ecclesiastical history of Ireland*. 4 vols. Dublin, 1829.

Liestol, Aslak. 'Rune'. In Fenton and Palsson (eds), *The northern and western isles in the Viking world*.

Lowe, Andy. The Holy Island architectural competition. In *Holy Island Project Newsletter, 1993*.

Lucas, A. T. The sacred trees of Ireland. In *Cork Hist. Soc. Jn.*, lxviii, (1963).

MacCana, Pronsias. *Celtic mythology*. London, 1970.

MacDonald, George and MacLeod, Fiona. *The gold key and the green life: some fantasies and Celtic tales*. Ed. Eliz. Sutherland. London, 1986.

Mac Innes, D. *Folk and hero tales*. Argyllshire series, ii. London, 1890.

Mackenzie, W. M. *The Book of Arran, vol. 2*. Glasgow, 1914. Brodick, 1982.

Mackinlay, J. M. '*In Oceana Desertum*' — Celtic anchorites and their island retreats. In *P.S.A.S.*, xxxiii (1898-9).

Mac Neill, Máire. *The festival of Lughnasa: a study of the survival of the Celtic festival of the beginning of the harvest*. Dublin, 1982.

MacSuibhne, P. *Cluain na nGall*. Carlow, 1975.

Mann, Horace. *Lives of the popes in the early Middle Ages*. London, 1925.

Martin, Angus. *Kintyre: the hidden past*. Edinburgh, 1984.

Martin, Martin. *A description of the western isles of Scotland*. Written c. 1695 but publ. Edinburgh & London, 1703.

McArthur, John. *The antiquities of Arran, with a historical sketch of the island, embracing an account of the Sudreyjar under the Norsemen.* Glasgow, 1861. 2nd ed., Edinburgh, 1873.

McCarthy, Thom. Destiny of Holy Island. In *Holy Island Project Newsletter.* 1993.

McCone, Kim. A tale of two ditties: poet and satirist in Cath Maige Tuired. In O Corráin. *Sages, saints and storytellers.*

McCone, Kim. Werewolves, cyclopes, díberga and fianna: juvenile delinquency in early Ireland. In *Cambridge Mediev. Celt. Studies,* xii (1986).

McDonald, R. Andrew. *The kingdom of the isles: Scotland's western seaboard c.1100-c.1336.* East Linton, 1996.

McLellan, Robert. *Ancient monuments of Arran.* Edinburgh, 1977.

McLellan, Robert. *Isle of Arran.* Ed. by Norman Newton, Devon, 1995.

McRoberts, David. Hermits in medieval Scotland. In *Innes Review,* xvi (1965).

Megaw, Basil. Norsemen and native in the kingdom of the isles. In *Scot. Studies,* xx (1976).

Merton, Thomas. *The Asian Journal of Thomas Merton.* Edited from his original notebooks by Naomi Burton, Bro. Patrick Hart and James Laughlin. London, 1974.

Meyer, Kuno. Early relations between Gael and Brython. Paper read to the Society of Cymmrodorian, 28 May 1896. No date or place of publication but a copy at Nat. Lib. Ire., P2047, no. 7, p.39.

Meyer, Kuno (ed.), *Ancient Irish poetry.* London, 1913.

Michelli, Perette. Four Scottish crosses and their relation to the Irish tradition. In *P.S.A.S.,* cxvi (1986)

Miller, W. *The Barrow Valley and its history, 1600-1750.* Carlow, n. d.

Milne, Allan. *Arran: an island's story.* Brodick, 1982.

Milner, J. E. *The tree book.* London, 1992.

Mitchell, Anthony. *The story of the church in Scotland.* Edinburgh, 1957.

Monro, Donald. *A description of the western isles of Scotland, called Hybrides...1549.* Edinburgh, 1774. Also in *Misc. Scot.,* ii.

Moore, Donald (ed.). *The Irish sea province in archaeology and history.* Cardiff, 1970.

Moran, Peter. Early Irish missionaries in Britain. In *Ossory Arch. Soc. Trans.,* i (1874-79).

Morley, Henry. *Ireland under Elizabeth and James I.* London, 1890.

Morris, J. *The age of Arthur: a history of the British Isles from 350 to 650.* London, 1973.

Muir, Thomas. *Ecclesiological notes on some of the islands of Scotland.* Edinburgh, 1885.

Murphy, Gerard. *Early Irish lyrics.* Oxford, 1956.

Murray, Patrick. Wooden vessel from Torr Righ, Shiskine. In *P.S.A.S.,* xxxvi (1902).

Nagy, J. F. The wisdom of the geilt. In *Éigse,* xix (1982-3).

Nagy, J. F. *The wisdom of the outlaw: the boyhood deeds of Finn in Gaelic narrative tradition*. Berkeley and London, 1985.

Nagy, J. F. *A new introduction to Buile Suibhne, the frenzy of Suibhne: being the adventures of Suighne Geilt: a middle-Irish romance*. Irish Texts Soc. London, 1996.

Neary, John. Pilgrimages to sacred wells. In *Ir. Eccles. Rec.*, series 5, xxvii (1920).

Nelson, E. C. and Walsh, Wendy. *Trees of Ireland: native and naturalised*. Dublin, 1993.

O Baóill, Colm. *Contributions to a comparative study of Ulster Irish and Scottish Gaelic*. Belfast, 1978.

O'Brien, M. A. A middle-Irish poem on the birth of Aedán Mac Gabráin and Brandub Mac Echach. In *Ériu*, xvi (1952).

O Corráin, Donnchadh et al. *Sages, saints and storytellers: Celtic studies in honour of Prof. James Carney*. Maynooth, 1989.

O Corráin, Donnchadh (ed.). *Irish antiquity: essays and studies presented to Prof. M. J. O'Kelly*. Dublin, 1994.

O Cróinín, Dáibhí. *Early medieval Ireland, 400-1200*. London and New York, 1995.

O'Dwyer, Peter. *Céli Dé: spiritual reform in Ireland 750-900*. 2nd ed., Dublin, 1981.

Olsen, Magnus. Runic inscriptions in Great Britain, Ireland and the Isle of Man. In Sketelig (ed.), *Viking Antiquities*.

O'Rahilly, T. F. On the origin of the names Érainn and Ériu. In *Ériu*, xiv (1943-6).

O'Rahilly, T. F. *Early Irish history and mythology*. Dublin, 1976.

O'Sullivan, T. F. Pattern day at St Moling's. In *Carloviana*, n. s., ii (1976/77).

O'Toole, Edward. The Holy wells of Co. Carlow. In *Béaloideas: the journal of the Folklore Society of Ireland*, iv, no. 4 (1934).

O'Toole, Edward. *Leighlin diocese: its ancient boundaries and divisions*. Carlow, 1936.

Pennant, Thomas. *A tour in Scotland and voyage to the Hebrides*. Chester, 1772.

[Perrott, David]. *Guide to the western islands of Scotland*. Edinburgh, 1986.

Picard, Jean-Michel . The strange death of Guaire Mac Aedáin. In O Corráin, *Sages, saints and storytellers*.

Pinkerton, John. *An enquiry into the history of Scotland*. 2 vols. New ed., Edinburgh, 1814.

Pokorny, Julius. Eine altirische legende aus dem Buch von Leinster. In Bergin and Marstrander, *Miscellany*.

Pokorny, Julius. Altirische texte. In *Zeitschrift Celt. Philologie*, ix (1913).

Robertson, James. Tour through some of the western islands, etc., of Scotland in 1768. In *P.S.A.S.*, xxxii (1898).

Roger, J. C. Notes on two additional runic ristings in St Molio's Cave, Holy Island, Lamlash Bay, Island of Arran. In *P.S.A.S.*, xix (1884-5).

Richards, Melville. Places and persons of the early Welsh church. In *Welsh Hist. Rev.*, xx (1970).

Ryan, John. *History and antiquities of the county of Carlow*. Dublin, 1833.

Scott, William. John of Fordun's description of the western isles. In *Scot. Studies*, xxiii (1979)

Sellar, W. D. H. The origin and ancestry of Somerled. In *S.H.R.*, xlv (1966).

Sharp, William. The Isle of Arran. In *Art Journal*, xlvii (July 1885).

Sharp, William. Cathal of the woods. In Macdonald and Macleod, *Gold key and green life*,

Shaw, R. Cunliffe. *The men of the north*. Lancashire, [1973].

Shirley, E. P. *Some account of the dominion of Farney in the province and earldom of Ulster*. London, 1845.

Shirley, E. P. *History of the county of Monaghan*. London, 1879.

Skene, William. *The coronation stone* [of Scone]. Edinburgh, 1869.

Skene, William. *Celtic Scotland: a history of ancient Alban*. 3 vols, Edinburgh, 1876-80.

Smyth, Alfred P. *Celtic Leinster*. Dublin, 1982.

Stevenson, David. The Irish Franciscan mission to Scotland and the Irish rebellion of 1641. In *Innes Review*, xxx (1979).

Stokes, George. Island monasteries of Wales and Ireland. In *R.S.A.I. Jn.*, series 5, i (1891)

Stokes, Whitley (ed.). The death of the sons of Uisneach. In *Irische Texte*, ii. Leipzig, 1884.

Stokes, Whitley (ed.). *The tripartite Life of Patrick*. 2 vols, London, 1887.

Stokes, Whitley (ed.). *The Edinburgh Dinnshenchas*. London, [1893].

Thomas, Charles. *Britain and Ireland in early Christian times, AD 400-800*. London, 1971.

Thompson, Caro. 'The dream that came true on Holy Island'. Unidentified London magazine article, c. December 1983 [thanks to Colin Cowley].

Thompson, Derin. *The companion to Gaelic Scotland*. Glasgow, 1994.

Thompson, Francis. *Highlands and islands of Scotland*. London, 1974.

Waddell, P. Hately. *Ossian and the Clyde: Fingal in Ireland*. Glasgow, 1875.

Waddell, John. Irish bronze age cists: a survey. In JRSAI, c (1970).

Wainright, F. T. (ed.). *The problem of the Picts*. Edinburgh, 1955.

W[akefield?], W.F. Leighlin cathedral. In *Ir. Eccl. Jn.*, (1 July 1851).

Walton, R. D. *Seventy walks in Arran*. Castle Douglas, n. d. [c.1976].

Ware, James. *Antiquities of Ireland*. First ed. in Latin, London, 1654 and accurate English translation, Dublin, 1705.

Ware, James. 'Annals', 'Antiquities', 'Bishops', etc. In Ware, *Antiquities*.

Ware, James. *Works concerning Ireland, revised and improved*. Ed. W. Harris. 2 vols, Dublin, 1739 and 1745.

Whaling, F. and Holmes, K, (eds). *The Samye symposia: no.1:1988: compassion through understanding*. Eskdalemuir, 1990.

Williams, Ronald. *The lords of the isles: the clan Donald and the early kingdom of the Scots*. London, 1984.

Wilson, Daniel. *The archaeology and prehistoric annals of Scotland*. Edinburgh, 1851.

Wilson, Daniel. Holy island and the runic inscriptions of St Molio's Cave, County of Bute. In *P.S.A.S.*, xvii (1882-3).

Index